Robert Fulghum was born in 1937 in Waco, Texas. He has several academic degrees, but, as he says, 'they aren't very important in comparison to the education I've gotten on my own.'

Throughout college and graduate school, Fulghum worked as a singing cowboy in guest ranches in Texas, Colorado and Montana, and rode in local rodeos. He has also found employment as an IBM salesperson, a bartender, and a folk music teacher. He plays guitar, bass and mando'cello. He is an accomplished painter and has had several successful showings of his work. For the past twenty years he has taught drawing and painting at the Lakeside School in Seattle.

For twenty-five years, he was also an ordained parish minister at Seattle's Edmonds Unitarian Church, where he is now minister emeritus. Fulghum has travelled twice around the world, living for a time in Thailand, Greece, Japan (in a Zen Buddhist monastery) and France. He now lives on a houseboat in Seattle and spends his leisure time sailing.

ROBERT FULGHUM

All I Really Need to Know I Learned in Kindergarten

Uncommon thoughts on common things

GRAFTON BOOKS
A Division of the Collins Publishing Group

LONDON GLASGOW
TORONTO SYDNEY AUCKLAND

Grafton Books
A Division of the Collins Publishing Group
8 Grafton Street, London W1X 3LA

Published in paperback by Grafton Books 1990

First published in Great Britain by
Grafton Books 1989

ISBN 0-586-20892-5

Printed and bound in Great Britain by
Collins, Glasgow

Set in Times

A portion of this text was originally published
in *Kansas City Times*

TO THE READER FROM THE AUTHOR

Before you move on, let me tell you just a few things. Give you a small map, in case you get lost.

What you are about to read was written over many years, a little bit at a time, and addressed to friends, family, a religious community, and myself, with no thought of publication in book form. I don't know what to call it. I think of it as "my stuff"—a written report about what goes on in my head and life.

A part of this—the part about what I learned in kindergarten—was passed around the country until it took on a life of its own. One day it was sent home from school in the knapsack of a child whose mother is a literary agent, and she wrote to me: Did I have anything else I had written? Well, yes. And one thing led to another in a Wonderland sort of way.

So here's more "stuff"—in a book—pretty much as it was written. I did change some names and facts to protect those who are either innocent or crabby or both.

And another thing: There are contradictions in here. You may be reading along and think, "Didn't he just say the opposite of that a few pages back?" Yes. It's just that I seem to hold in my head some mutually exclusive notions. For example, it is true that the unexamined life is not worth living, and true that ignorance is bliss, and so on. I haven't made up my mind about everything yet.

What else to tell you?

Read it a little bit at a time—there's no hurry and no resolution of the plot at the end.

Finally, I should tell you that I have an official Storyteller's License. A friend made it up and taped it to the wall over my desk. This license gives me permission to use my imagination in rearranging my experience to improve a story, so long as it serves some notion of Truth. It also contains the Storyteller's Creed:

I believe that imagination is stronger than knowledge.
That myth is more potent than history.
That dreams are more powerful than facts.
That hope always triumphs over experience.
That laughter is the only cure for grief.
And I believe that love is stronger than death.

I have tried very hard not to write anything that would cause my license to be revoked.

—Robert Fulghum

ALL I REALLY NEED TO KNOW I LEARNED IN KINDERGARTEN

EACH SPRING, FOR MANY YEARS, I have set myself the task of writing a personal statement of belief: a Credo. When I was younger, the statement ran for many pages, trying to cover every base, with no loose ends. It sounded like a Supreme Court brief, as if words could resolve all conflicts about the meaning of existence.

The Credo has grown shorter in recent years— sometimes cynical, sometimes comical, sometimes bland—but I keep working at it. Recently I set out to get the statement of personal belief down to one page in simple terms, fully understanding the naïve idealism that implied.

The inspiration for brevity came to me at a gasoline station. I managed to fill an old car's tank with super-deluxe high-octane go-juice. My old hoopy couldn't handle it and got the willies—kept sputtering out at intersections and belching going downhill. I understood. My mind and my spirit get like that from time to time. Too much high-content information, and *I* get the existential willies—keep sputtering out at intersections where life choices must be made and I either know too much or not enough. The examined life is no picnic.

I realized then that I already know most of what's necessary to live a meaningful life—that it isn't all that complicated. *I know it*. And have known it for a long, long time. Living it—well, that's another matter, yes? Here's my Credo:

ALL I REALLY NEED TO KNOW about how to live and what to do and how to be I learned in kindergarten. Wisdom was not at the top of the graduate-school mountain, but there in the sandpile at Sunday School. These are the things I learned:

Share everything.
Play fair.
Don't hit people.
Put things back where you found them.
Clean up your own mess.
Don't take things that aren't yours.
Say you're sorry when you hurt somebody.
Wash your hands before you eat.
Flush.
Warm cookies and cold milk are good for you.
Live a balanced life—learn some and think some

and draw and paint and sing and dance and play and work every day some.

Take a nap every afternoon.

When you go out into the world, watch out for traffic, hold hands, and stick together.

Be aware of wonder. Remember the little seed in the Styrofoam cup: The roots go down and the plant goes up and nobody really knows how or why, but we are all like that.

Goldfish and hamsters and white mice and even the little seed in the Styrofoam cup—they all die. So do we.

And then remember the Dick-and-Jane books and the first word you learned—the biggest word of all—LOOK.

Everything you need to know is in there some-where. The Golden Rule and love and basic sanita-tion. Ecology and politics and equality and sane living.

Take any one of those items and extrapolate it into sophisticated adult terms and apply it to your family life or your work or your government or your world and it holds true and clear and firm. Think what a better world it would be if we all—the whole world—had cookies and milk about three o'clock every after-noon and then lay down with our blankies for a nap. Or if all governments had as a basic policy to always put things back where they found them and to clean up their own mess.

And it is still true, no matter how old you are—when you go out into the world, it is best to hold hands and stick together.

I AM IN CHARGE OF THE LAUNDRY at our house. I like my work. It gives me a sense of accomplishment. And a feeling of involvement with the rest of the family, in a way. And time alone in the back room, without the rest of the family, which is also nice, sometimes.

I like sorting the clothes—lights, darks, in-betweens. I like setting the dials—hot, cold, rinse, time, heat. These are choices I can understand and make with decisive skill. I still haven't figured out the new stereo, but washers and dryers I can handle. The bell dings—you pull out the warm, fluffy clothes, take them to the dining-room table, sort and fold them into neat piles. I especially like it when there's lots of static electricity, and you can hang socks all over your body and they will stick there. (*My wife caught me doing this once and gave me THAT LOOK. You can't always explain everything you do to everybody, you know.*)

When I'm finished, I have a sense of accomplishment. A sense of competence. I am good at doing the laundry. At *least* that. And it's a religious experience, you know. Water, earth, fire—polarities of wet and dry, hot and cold, dirty and clean. The great cycles—round and round—beginning and end—Alpha and Omega, amen. I am in touch with the GREAT SOME-THING-OR-OTHER. For a moment, at least, life is tidy and has meaning. But then, again . . .

The washing machine died last week. Guess I overloaded it with towels. And the load got all lumped up on one side during the spin cycle. So it did this incredible herky-jerky, lurching dance across the floor and blew itself up. I thought it was coming for me. One minute it was a living thing in the throes of a seizure, and the next minute a cold white box full of partially digested towels with froth around its mouth, because I guess I must have fed it too much soap, too. Five minutes later the dryer expired. Like a couple of elderly folks in a nursing home who follow one another quickly in death, so closely are they entwined.

It was Saturday afternoon, and all the towels in the house were wet, and all my shorts and socks were wet, and now what? Knowing full well that if you want one of those repair guys you have to stay home for thirty-six hours straight and have your banker standing by with a certified check or else they won't set foot on your property, and I haven't got time for that. So it's the laundromat over at the mall.

Now I haven't spent a Saturday night in the laundromat since I was in college. What you miss by not going to laundromats anymore are things like seeing other people's clothes and overhearing conversations you'd never hear anywhere else. I watched an old lady sort out a lot of sexy black underwear and wondered if it was hers or not. And heard a college kid explain to a friend how to get puke off a suede jacket.

Sitting there waiting, I contemplated the detergent box. I use Cheer. I like the idea of a happy wash. Sitting there late at night, leaning against the dryer for warmth, eating a little cheese and crackers and drinking a little white wine out of the thermos (*I came prepared*), I got to brooding about the meaning of life and started reading the stuff on the Cheer box. Amazing. It contains ingredients to lift dirt from clothes (anionic surfactants) and soften water (complex sodium phosphates). Also, agents to protect washer parts (sodium silicate) and improve processing (sodium sulfate), small quantities of stuff to reduce wrinkling and prevent fabric yellowing, plus whiteners, colorant, and perfume. No kidding. All this for less than a nickel an ounce. It's biodegradable and works best in cold water—ecologically sound. A miracle in a box.

Sitting there watching the laundry go around in the dryer, I thought about the round world and hygiene. We've made a lot of progress, you know. We used to think that disease was an act of God. Then we figured out it was a product of human ignorance, so we've been cleaning up our act—literally—ever since. We've been getting the excrement off our hands and clothes and bodies and food and houses.

If only the scientific experts could come up with something to get it out of our minds. One cup of fixit frizzle that will lift the dirt from our lives, soften our hardness, protect our inner parts, improve our processing, reduce our yellowing and wrinkling, improve our natural color, and make us sweet and good.

Don't try Cheer, by the way. I tasted it. It's awful. *(But my tongue is clean, now.)*

THIS IS MY NEIGHBOR. Nice lady. Coming out her front door, on her way to work and in her "looking good" mode. She's locking the door now and picking up her daily luggage: purse, lunch bag, gym bag for aerobics, and the garbage bucket to take out. She turns, sees me, gives me the big, smiling Hello, takes three steps across her front porch. And goes "AAAAAAAAGGGGGGGGGGHHHHHHHHHH!!!!" (*That's a direct quote.*) At about the level of a fire engine at full cry. Spider web! She has walked full force into a spider web. And the pressing question, of course: Just where is the spider *now*?

She flings her baggage in all directions. And at the same time does a high-kick, jitterbug sort of dance— like a mating stork in crazed heat. Clutches at her face and hair and goes "AAAAAAAGGGGGGGGHHHH-HHHHH!!!!!" at a new level of intensity. Tries opening the front door without unlocking it. Tries again.

Breaks key in the lock. Runs around the house headed for the back door. Doppler effect of

"A A A A A G G G H H H H a a g g h . . ."

Now a different view of this scene. Here is the spider. Rather ordinary, medium gray, middle-aged lady spider. She's been up since before dawn working on her web, and all is well. Nice day, no wind, dew point just right to keep things sticky. She's out checking the moorings and thinking about the little gnats she'd like to have for breakfast. Feeling good. Ready for action. All of a sudden all hell breaks loose—earthquake, tornado, volcano. The web is torn loose and is wrapped around a frenzied moving haystack, and a huge piece of raw-but-painted meat is making a sound the spider never heard before: "AAAAAAAG-GGGGGGGGHHHHHHHHH!!!!!!" It's too big to wrap up and eat later, and it's moving too much to hold down. Jump for it? Hang on and hope? Dig in?

Human being. She has caught a human being. And the pressing question is, of course: Where is it going and what will it do when it gets there?

The neighbor lady thinks the spider is about the size of a lobster and has big rubber lips and poisonous fangs. The neighbor lady will probably strip to the skin and take a full shower and shampoo just to make sure it's gone—and then put on a whole new outfit to make certain she is not inhabited.

The spider? Well, if she survives all this, she will really have something to talk about—the one that got away that was THIS BIG. "And you should have seen the JAWS on the thing!"

Spiders. Amazing creatures. Been around maybe 350 million years, so they can cope with about anything. Lots of them, too—sixty or seventy thousand per suburban acre. It's the web thing that I envy. Imagine what it would be like if people were equipped like spiders. If we had this little six-nozzled aperture right at the base of our spine and we could make yards of something like glass fiber with it. Wrapping packages would be a cinch! Mountain climbing would never be the same. Think of the Olympic events. And mating and child rearing would take on new dimensions. Well, you take it from there. It boggles the mind. Cleaning up human-sized webs would be a mess, on the other hand.

All this reminds me of a song I know. And you know, too. And your parents and your children, they know. About the eensy-weensy spider. Went up the waterspout. Down came the rain and washed the spider out. Out came the sun and dried up all the rain. And the eensy-weensy spider went up the spout again. You probably know the motions, too.

What's the deal here? Why do we all know that song? Why do we keep passing it on to our kids? Especially when it puts spiders in such a favorable

light? Nobody goes "AAAAAAAGGGGGGGGHH-
HHHHHHH!!!!!" when they sing it. Maybe because
it puts the life adventure in such clear and simple
terms. The small creature is alive and looks for adventure. Here's the drainpipe—a long tunnel going
up toward some light. The spider doesn't even think
about it—just goes. Disaster befalls it—rain, flood,
powerful forces. And the spider is knocked down and
out beyond where it started. Does the spider say, "To
hell with that"? No. Sun comes out—clears things
up—dries off the spider. And the small creature goes
over to the drainpipe and looks up and thinks it *really*
wants to know what is up there. It's a little wiser
now—checks the sky first, looks for better toeholds,
says a spider prayer, and heads up through mystery
toward the light and wherever.

Living things have been doing just that for a long,
long time. Through every kind of disaster and set-
back and catastrophe. We are survivors. And we teach
our kids about that. And maybe spiders tell their kids
about it, too, in their spider sort of way.

So the neighbor lady will survive and be a little
wiser coming out the door on her way to work. And
the spider, if it lives, will do likewise. And if not,
well, there are lots more spiders, and the word gets
around. Especially when the word is "AAAAAAA-
GGGGGGGGGHHHHHHHHH!!!!"

*I*N THE SOLOMON ISLANDS IN THE SOUTH PACIFIC some villagers practice a unique form of logging. If a tree is too large to be felled with an ax, the natives cut it down by yelling at it. *(Can't lay my hands on the article, but I swear I read it.)* Woodsmen with special powers creep up on a tree just at dawn and suddenly scream at it at the top of their lungs. They continue this for thirty days. The tree dies and falls over. The theory is that the hollering kills the spirit of the tree. According to the villagers, it always works.

Ah, those poor naïve innocents. Such quaintly charming habits of the jungle. Screaming at trees, indeed. How primitive. Too bad they don't have the advantages of modern technology and the scientific mind.

Me? I yell at my wife. And yell at the telephone and the lawn mower. And yell at the TV and the newspaper and my children. I've even been known to shake my fist and yell at the sky at times.

Man next door yells at his car a lot. And this summer I heard him yell at a stepladder for most of an afternoon. We modern, urban, educated folks yell at traffic and umpires and bills and banks and machines— especially machines. Machines and relatives get most of the yelling.

Don't know what good it does. Machines and things just sit there. Even kicking doesn't always help. As for people, well, the Solomon Islanders may have a point. Yelling at living things does tend to kill the spirit in them. Sticks and stones may break our bones, but words will break our hearts. . . .

*E*VER SEEN AN ABACUS? You know, those centi-pedelike things with wooden beads in rows. They're sold mostly in knickknack import shops, for wall decoration. But, in fact, an abacus is an adding machine, calculator, and computer. On second thought, that's not quite true. The abacus is just a visual record of the computations going on in the mind of the person using it.

Millions of people in Asia still use the abacus daily. And it has been in use there for a couple of thousand years or more. Not only is it an effective practical tool, but it is nice to look at. Nice to hold and touch. Wood and brass and ivory. And the older they get and the longer they are handled by a human being, the lovelier they get—smooth and dark and polished. They will last for a lifetime; they will never need updating; all the software needed to drive them is between your ears; and if they break they can be fixed by an eight-year-old with household tools.

The presence of the abacus puts some kinds of progress in perspective. I remember a time when a Japanese-American computer conglomerate moved into the Chinese market in a big way. In order to demonstrate the value of its small pocket calculators, it arranged a contest. The great abacus-PC shoot-out. The guy who won—the one with the abacus, of course—was named Chan Kai Kit. Hong Kong Chinese—a senior clerk for a shipping company. It is true that the operator of the little computer did handle the pile of invoices forty-four seconds faster than Chan Kai Kit and his abacus. But the computer got the wrong answer. Seems the machine operator was in too big a hurry to prove how smart his machine was and fed it fuzzy facts. Much face was lost.

Now don't get me wrong. Pocket calculators are here to stay, and they have their place. A Luddite I am not—machines are not evil in themselves. And a careful, thoughtful man like Chan Kai Kit might do even better with his own pocket calculator instead of his abacus—who knows? It's just that I'm a sentimentalist about the wonders of the human hand and mind. And when I find evidence that it can still hold its own in the face of the wizardry of the electronic circuitry of little chips, I am pleased. It is comforting to know that some very old and very simple ways of getting from one place to another still work.

And I ponder the fact that an ancient and worn

abacus will find its way to the walls of the twentieth century as a thing of art and wonder, made lovely by its usefulness and made useful by its beauty. I have an old wooden bowl and an elderly chopping knife I would stack up against a food processor any day. It's the same story.

*I*N LATE APRIL OF 1757, SOLDIERS under Colonel Diego Ortiz de Parilla and five priests set out from San Antonio, bound for a spot on the San Saba River in the hill country of central Tejas (that's Texas, gringo). They came to extend Spanish influence; to bring Christianity to whatever heathens they might come upon. Also, they came to destroy the Apache Indians (after converting them, of course). Above all, they came to search for treasure said to be hidden in the hills of the Balcones Escarpment.

Built a fort, they did, and a mission chapel, too. And waited for the Indians to come to them for comfort and solace, with treasure. While they bided their time, they wrote journals, still extant in the library down at Austin. "The country fills my spirit with its simple beauty," said Padre Molina, "but where are the Indians?" Diego Ortiz de Parilla said, "The country is good, but where are the Indians, and where is the treasure?"

24

The answer to some of the questions came the following March. When two thousand Comanches (invited by the Apaches) showed up in red-and-black war paint, with malice on their minds.

San Saba was a kind of quiet place for a while after that. The fort, the mission, and most of the adventuresome *hidalgos* were wiped from the face of the earth. And, treasureless, the remnant straggled back to San Antonio, never to return.

Information to that effect was engraved on the historical marker I read in the town square in San Saba this spring. It was supplemented by a pair of elderly gentlemen sitting-and-spitting on a bench in front of the old courthouse. As it was explained to me, the Texans whipped the Mexicans and the Indians and took over what was rightfully theirs. And San Saba, Texas, is a right peaceful place now. "Pecan and Goat Capital of the World." So says *The San Saba News & Star*, which has been publishing for 111 years.

The reason I was in San Saba was just to touch base. Used to travel down from Waco on weekends to court a lady friend named Louise. And long after Louise had had the bad judgment to take up with someone else, I still went down to San Saba weekends. For one thing, I could buy beer there. My county was dry, as only a county filled with Baptists could be. And for another, they had a little rodeo that featured goat-roping, and goat-roping is *some* entertainment. Goats don't break out of the chute running for the pen at the other end. They move like they are crazed. Waltz out of the chute, flash left, dead stop, run back toward the roper. And they try to butt you when you try to tie them down. You never know about goats. It's worth going a long way to see goat-roping. And get some beer. When you're eighteen. And Louise might have changed her mind.

Too, there was a dance afterward out in the open air on a concrete slab alongside the San Saba River. And you could sit there in peace and watch the dancing and the river and eat a baloney-and-white-bread sandwich with a whole bag of Fritos and a whole bag of chocolate cookies washed down with a six-pack of Lone Star. Then you'd go dance and hope to God you didn't throw up.

San Saba, Texas. A piece of home. And it hasn't changed much, which is why I was there this spring. The Spaniards and the Indians are a long way gone over in one direction of time. And the Interstate and the shopping malls of New Texas are a long way over in another. Nothing left but Texas stuck somewhere in time about 1945. The big excitement in town is that the San Saba Armadillos high school basketball team is going to the state finals. And the new Kingdom Hall of Jehovah's Witnesses burned down. Some said it was the Methodists, but I don't know.

This latter information I overheard at the soda fountain at Bob Everett's Drugstore on the square.

Had a Coke float for thirty-five cents and backed that up with apple pie made by Miz Bob and some hundred-mile coffee—all for eighty-nine cents. Then over to Harry's Store to get into a new pair of Tony Lama calfskin boots with goat-roping heels. Wrote them a check—out-of-town check—and they didn't even ask to see my I.D. Figured I needed the boots. Lady said not many people come all the way from Seattle to buy boots, and she figured I was either honest or stupid and she'd bet on honest.

Then over to the feedstore on the square for some real deerskin roping gloves. Best work gloves in the world. New roping gloves smell like nothing else, and if they fit just right it takes a surgeon to get them off. And then out to the Commission Company to watch the regular Friday afternoon goat and sheep auction. Almost bought a goat, too. Goats are real cheap in San Saba—about twenty dollars gets a little one. I like goats.

It's real quiet there at night, in San Saba, Texas. After you eat your chicken-fried steak with country gravy with a side of succotash and mashed potatoes, you stick a wintergreen toothpick between your teeth and wander out the front door of the Alamo Cafe and around the courthouse square to the edge of the river, and you can't hear a thing except crickets and spring frogs. And the same is true for all those little towns scattered across central Texas—Cranfils Gap, China

Springs, Valley Mills. Quiet. Very quiet, come sun-down. Quiet and old and simple and ordinary and very real. A piece of home.

I know. You think I'm making this all up. But I'm not. It's true. Most of it. And no, it's *not* heaven on earth. It's boring as hell in its own way, and I wouldn't want to live there a week. So why do I tell you, anyway? It's just this: that there are places we all come from—deep-rooty-common places—that make us who we are. And we disdain them or treat them lightly at our peril. We turn our backs on them at the risk of self-contempt. There is a sense in which we need to go home again—and can go home again. Not to recover home, no. But to sanctify memory.

The Spaniards were right about one thing. About San Saba, I mean. Though hard it is to explain, the old legend was correct. There is treasure there.

THE RUSSIANS ARE A ROTTEN LOT, immoral, aggressive, ruthless, coarse, and generally evil. They are responsible for most of the troubles in this world. They're not like us.

That's pretty much the summary of the daily news about the Russians. But sometimes something slips through the net of prejudice, some small bit of a sign that is so clean and true and real that it wedges open the rusting Iron Curtain long enough for us to see not an enemy but fellow travelers, joined to us by membership in the Fellowship of Joy-and-Pain.

See Nicolai Pestretsov. I don't know much about him, I don't know where he is now, but I'll tell you what I know.

He was a sergeant major in the Russian army, thirty-six years old. He was stationed in Angola, a long way from home. His wife had come out to visit him.

On August 24, South African military units entered

31

Angola in an offensive against the black nationalist guerrillas taking sanctuary there. At the village of N-Giva, they encountered a group of Russian soldiers. Four were killed and the rest of the Russians fled—except for Sergeant Major Pestretsov. He was captured, as we know because the South African military communiqué said: "Sgt. Major Nicolai Pestretsov refused to leave the body of his slain wife, who was killed in the assault on the village."

It was as if the South Africans could not believe it, for the communiqué repeated the information. "He went to the body of his wife and would not leave it, although she was dead."

How strange. Why didn't he run and save his own hide? What made him go back? Is it possible that he loved her? Is it possible that he wanted to hold her in his arms one last time? Is it possible that he needed to cry and grieve? Is it possible that he felt the stupidity of war? Is it possible that he felt the injustice of fate? Is it possible that he thought of children, born or unborn? Is it possible that he didn't care what became of him now?

It's possible. We don't know. Or at least we don't know for certain. But we can guess. His actions answer.

And so he sits alone in a South African prison. Not a "Russian" or "Communist" or "soldier" or "enemy" or any of those categories. Just-a-man who cared for just-a-woman for just-a-time more than anything else.

Here's to you, Nicolai Pestretsov, wherever you may go and be, for giving powerful meaning to the promises that are the same everywhere; for dignifying that covenant that is the same in any language—"for better or for worse, in good times and in bad, in sickness and in health, to love and honor and cherish unto death, so help me God." You kept the faith; kept it bright—kept it shining. Bless you!

(Oh, the Russians are a rotten lot, immoral, aggressive, ruthless, coarse, and generally evil. They are responsible for most of the troubles of this world. They are not like us.)

Sure.

THIS IS KIND OF PERSONAL. It may get a little syrupy, so watch out. It started as a note to my wife. And then I thought that since some of you might have husbands or wives and might feel the same way, I'd pass it along. I don't own this story, anyway. Charles Boyer does.

Remember Charles Boyer? Suave, dapper, handsome, graceful. Lover of the most famous and beautiful ladies of the silver screen. That was on camera and in the fan magazines. In real life it was different.

There was only one woman. For forty-four years. His wife, Patricia. Friends said it was a lifelong love affair. They were no less lovers and friends and companions after forty-four years than after the first year.

Then Patricia developed cancer of the liver. And though the doctors told Charles, he could not bear to tell her. And so he sat by her bedside to provide hope and cheer. Day and night for six months. He could not change the inevitable. Nobody could. And Patricia died in his arms. Two days later Charles Boyer was also dead. By his own hand. He said he did not want to live without her. He said, "Her love was life to me."

This was no movie. As I said, it's the real story—Charles Boyer's story.

It's not for me to pass judgment on how he handled his grief. But it is for me to say that I am touched and comforted in a strange way. Touched by the depth of love behind the apparent sham of Hollywood love life. Comforted to know that a man and woman can love each other that much that long.

I don't know how I would handle my grief in similar circumstances. I pray I shall never have to stand in his shoes. *(Here comes the personal part—no apologies.)* But there are moments when I look across the room—amid the daily ordinariness of life—and see the person I call my wife and friend and companion. And I understand why Charles Boyer did what he did. It really is possible to love someone that much. I know. I'm certain of it.

*W*ATCHED A MAN SETTING UP A VALENTINE'S DAY display in a store window. It's the middle of January, but the merchants need to get a jump on love, I guess. Don't get me wrong—merchants are fine folks. They give us choices and keep us informed on the important holidays. How would you know it was Halloween or Valentine's Day or Mother's Day early enough to do something about it, if merchants didn't stay on the job?

The other group I count on is kindergarten teachers. They always know about holidays, and when it comes to valentines and other evidence of love, no merchant can compete with them. What the kindergarten teachers set in motion, no merchant could sell—it's beyond price—you can't get it at the store.

What I'm talking about here is something I think of as the *gummy lump*. Once it was a shoe box, decorated and given to me by the oldest child. Then it became a repository of other relics of childhood given to me by the younger children. The shoebox became my treasure chest in time. Its components are standard: Three colors of construction paper—pink and red and white—faded now, aluminum foil, orange tissue paper, several paper doilies, three kinds of macaroni, gumdrops, jelly beans, some little white hearts (the kind that taste like Tums) with words on them, and the whole thing held together with a whole big lot of white library paste, which also tastes like Tums.

Anyhow, this shoe box isn't looking too very good now. It's a little shriveled and kind of moldy where the jelly beans and gumdrops have run together. It's still sticky in places, and most of it is more beige than red and white. If you lift the lid, however, you will begin to know what makes me keep it. On folded and faded and fragile pieces of large-lined school paper, there are words: "Hi daddi" and "Hoppy valimtime" and "I lov you." A whole big lot of "I lov you." Glued to the bottom of the box are twenty-three X's and O's made out of macaroni. I've counted them more than once. Also scrawled in several places are the names of three children.

The treasures of King Tut are nothing in the face of this.

Have you got something around the house like a gummy lump? Evidence of love in its most uncomplicated and most trustworthy state? You may live a

long, long time. You may receive gifts of great value
and beauty. You may experience much love. But you
will never believe in it quite as much as you believe in
the gummy lump. It makes your world go round and
the ride worth the trouble.

The three children are grown up now. They still
love me, though it's harder sometimes to get direct
evidence. And it's love that's complicated by age and
knowledge and confusing values. Love, to be sure.
But not simple. Not something you could put in a
shoe box.

This sticky icon sits on a shelf at the top of my
closet. Nobody else knows it's there. But I do. It is a
talisman, a kind of cairn to memory, and I think
about it every morning as I dress. Once in a while I
take it down from the shelf and open it. It is something I can touch and hold and believe in, especially
when love gets difficult and there are no small arms
around my neck anymore.

Oh, sure, this is the worst kind of simpleminded,
heartrending Daddy-drivel imaginable. I've probably
embarrassed us both by telling you. But its beats hell
out of a mood ring or a mantra when it comes to
comfort.

I have no apology. The gummy lump stands for
my kind of love. Bury it with me. I want to take it
with me as far as I go.

THIS IS ABOUT A HOUSE I ONCE LIVED IN. An elderly lakeside cottage built at the end of the road at the end of the nineteenth century. A summer place for a family who traveled by horse and buggy out from Seattle through deep woods and over steep hills on logging trails. It was wild there, then, and it is wild there still.

The house sat off the ground on bricks, surrounded by thickets of blackberry bushes and morning-glory vines bent on a struggle to the death. And even though it is only minutes, now, from downtown, squirrels, rabbits, feral pussycats, and "things" I never saw but only heard had long established squatters' rights on the property.

And raccoons. We had raccoons. Big ones. Several.

For reasons known only to God and the hormones of raccoons, they chose to mate underneath my house. Every spring. And for reasons known only to God and the hormones of raccoons, they chose to mate underneath my house at three A.M.

Until you have experienced raccoons mating underneath your bedroom at three in the morning, you have missed one of life's more sensational moments. It is an uncommon event, to say the least. If you've ever heard cats fighting in the night, you have a clue. Magnify the volume and the intensity by ten. It's not what you'd call a sensual and erotic sound. More like a three-alarm fire is what it is.

I remember the first time it happened. Since conditions were not really conducive to sleep, I got up. When I say I got up, I mean *I GOT UP*. About three feet. Straight up. Covers and all.

When I had recovered my aplomb and adjusted to the new adrenaline level, I got a flashlight and went outside and peered up under the house. This lady raccoon and her suitor were squared off in a corner, fangs bared, covered with mud and blood, and not looking very sexy at all.

Neither my presence nor the beam of light could override what drove them on. With snarls and barks and screams, the passionate encounter raged on. While I watched, the matter was finally consummated and resolved. They had no shame. What had to be done was done. And they wandered off, in a kind of glazy-eyed stupor, to groom themselves for whatever might come next in the life of a raccoon.

I sat there in the rain, my light still shining into the trysting chamber. And I pondered. Why is it that love and life so often have to be carried forth with so much pain and strain and mess? I ask you, why is that?

I was thinking of my own sweet wife asleep in the bed right above me, and our own noises of conflict mixed with affection. I wondered what the raccoons must conclude from the sounds a husband and wife make at night—the ones that sound like "If-you-really-loved-me-you-would-not-keep-making-such-a-mess-in-the-bathroom," followed by "OH, YEAH? WELL, LET ME TELL YOU A FEW THINGS. . . ."

Why isn't love easy?

I don't know. And the raccoons don't say.

CASSIDA RUBIGNOSA IS THE FORMAL NAME OF A beetle. In its larval form, it carries a small sack of garbage around on its back. There's a little pronged fork sticking up at the end of its abdomen. When the larva molts, the old skin catches on the fork and makes a kind of garbage bag. The anal aperture is right there, too, and fecal matter is deposited in the bag. For a long time, zoologists pondered the purpose of this arrangement.

Then they noticed the ant. A hunting ant that likes to eat beetle larvae. An ant that is also fastidious in nature, grooming itself often to keep tidy. *(You see what's coming?)*

So when the ant scurries up and gives the larva a preliminary feel to size it up for dinner, the larva hits it with the garbage bag. The ant falls back to clean up the noxious mess, and the larva slumps away. Zoologists refer to this device as a "fecal shield."

And while I have never actually seen this encounter take place (*I just read about it in a book, so it must be true. . . .*), it rings a bell.

I was at a cocktail party recently and saw a man and a woman doing the same thing as the larva and the ant.

Nature so works it that everybody gets a turn at getting what they deserve in one way or another. And while the meek may or may not be blessed, some of them are prepared.

LAWYER FRIEND MADE HIS ANNUAL SUMMER VISIT last week, up from California. Traveling with two eighteen-year-old girls and a small boa constrictor. In an anemic VW van with PEACE, LOVE, LIGHT written on the side. The inside of the bus was decorated like the set for *Alice in Wonderland*. He's forty-seven. Wife, four kids, house in the Berkeley hills, job in the city with big firm . . . the whole catastrophe.

I keep up with him because he's always a little ahead of the times. He's taken all the trips—and I do mean ALL the trips. A walking sociological experiment of the sixties and seventies in American culture. Civil rights, Vietnam, Hip, TA, TM, vegetarian, Zen, massage, LSD, palmistry, ten brands of yoga, macrame, psychoanalysis, backpacking, hot tubs, nudism, crystals, more religious movements than you can name, and vitamins. He's got all the equipment—blenders and pipes and grinders and bikes and jogging outfits and oils and unguents and grow lights—the works.

This year he is into simple ignorance. "It's all crap," says he. "All lies. Your senses lie to you, the president lies to you, the more you search the less you find, the more you try, the worse it gets. Ignorance is bliss. Just *BE,* man. Don't think or do—just *BE.* The *WORLD* is coming to an *END!*"

The day before he left, he jumped off a lakeside dock with his clothes on to help a kid who appeared to be in danger of drowning in the deep water. And he confessed to being in town for the National Lawyers Guild convention, since he's a member of its social justice committee.

"So, if it's all lies and crap—and ignorance is the ultimate trip—then how come . . . ?" I say.

"Well," says he, "*I might be wrong.*"

Pieces of sanity are found washed ashore on all kinds of beaches these days. And skepticism and realism are not the same as cynicism and pessimism. I mention it because it seems like a good bumper sticker for the eighties: "*I may be wrong.*"

GOOD FRIENDS FINALLY PUT THEIR RESOURCES together and made themselves a child. Me, I'm the godfather in the deal. I take my job seriously.

So far I've introduced the kid to the good things in life—chocolate, beer, cigars, Beethoven, and dirty jokes. I don't think he cares much for Beethoven. But he's only a year and a half old, and he'll get tired of chocolate, beer, cigars, and dirty jokes. I haven't told him about sex yet, but he's got some ideas of his own already. I won't go into details here, but if you have ever had a little kid or have ever been a little kid, then you know what I mean.

Also, I introduced him to crayons. Bought the Crayola beginner set—the short, fat, thick ones with training wheels. Every few weeks I would put one in his hand and show him how to make a mark with it. Mostly he just held it and stared at me. He had a cigar in his other hand and couldn't tell the difference be-

tween it and the Crayola. Then we went through the
orifice-stuffing phase, where the Crayola went in his
mouth and ears and nose. Finally, last week, I held his
hand and made a big red mark with the Crayola on a
sheet of newsprint. And *WHAM!* He got the picture.
A light bulb went off in a new room in his head. And
he did it again on his own. Now, reports his mother,
with a mixture of pleasure and pain, there is no stop-
ping him.

Crayolas plus imagination (the ability to create
images)—these make for happiness if you are a child.
Amazing things, Crayolas. Some petroleum-based
wax, some dye, a little binder—not much to them.
Until you add the imagination. The Binney Company in Pennsylvania makes about two billion of these
oleaginous sticks of pleasure every year and exports
them to every country in the United Nations. Crayolas are one of the few things the human race has in
common. That green-and-yellow box hasn't changed
since 1937. In fact, the only change has been to re-
name the "flesh" color "peach." That's a sign of
progress.

The way I know about "flesh" and "peach" is that,
when I bought my godson his trainer set, I indulged
myself. Bought my very own set of sixty-four. In the
big four-section box with the sharpener built right in.
Never had my own set before. Seems like I was always too young or too old to have one. While I was

at it, I bought several sets. Got one for the kid's mother and father and explained it was theirs, not his.

What I notice is that every adult or child I give a new set of Crayolas to goes a little funny. The kids smile, get a glazed look on their faces, pour the crayons out, and just look at them for a while. Then they go to work on the nearest flat surface and will draw anything you ask, just name it. The adults always get the most wonderful kind of sheepish smile on their faces—a mixture of delight and nostalgia and silliness. And they immediately start telling you about all their experiences with Crayolas. Their first box, using every color, breaking them, trying to get them in the box in order again, trying to use them in a bundle, putting them on hot things to see them melt, shaving them onto waxed paper and ironing them into stained glass windows, eating them, and on and on. If you want an interesting party sometime, combine cocktails and a fresh box of Crayolas for everybody.

When you think about it, for sheer bulk there's more art done with Crayolas than with anything else. There must be billions of sheets of paper in every country in the world, in billions of boxes and closets and attics and cupboards, covered with billions of pictures in crayon. The imagination of the human race poured out like a river. Ronald Reagan and Mikhail Gorbachev used crayons, I bet. So did Fidel and the emperor of Japan and Rajiv Gandhi and Mrs.

Thatcher and Mr. Mubarak and maybe even the aya-tollah. And just about everybody else you care to name.

Maybe we should develop a Crayola bomb as our next secret weapon. A happiness weapon. A Beauty Bomb. And every time a crisis developed, we would launch one. It would explode high in the air—explode softly—and send thousands, millions, of little para-chutes into the air. Floating down to earth—boxes of Crayolas. And we wouldn't go cheap, either—not little boxes of eight. Boxes of sixty-four, with the sharpener built right in. With silver and gold and copper, magenta and peach and lime, amber and um-ber and all the rest. And people would smile and get a little funny look on their faces and cover the world with imagination.

Guess that sounds absurd, doesn't it? A bit dumb. Crazy and silly and weird. But I was reading in the paper today how much money the Russians and our Congress just set aside for weapons. And I think about what those weapons will do. And I'm not con-fused about what's weird and silly and crazy and absurd. And I'm not confused about the lack of, or the need for, imagination in low or high places. Pass the crayons, please.

THE WINDING DOWN OF SUMMER puts me in a heavy philosophical mood. I am thinking about the deep, very private personal needs of people. Needs that when met give us a great sense of well-being. We don't like to talk about these for fear that people will not understand. But to increase our level of intimacy, I will tell you about one of mine: chicken-fried steak.

If you have any idea what's good, you already know you take a piece of stringy beef, pound hell out of it with a kitchen sledge, dip it in egg and flour, drop it in a skillet with bacon drippings, and fry it up. Then you take it out, throw in some flour and milk and salt and pepper, and you got serious gravy. On the plate with the steak you lay peas and mashed potatoes, and then dump on the gravy. Some cornbread and butter and a quart of cold milk on the side. Then you take knife and fork in hand, hunker down close to the trough, lift your eyes heavenward in praise of the wonders of the Lord, and don't stop until you've mopped up the last trace of gravy with the last piece of cornbread.

Disgusting, you say. Sure, but you probably eat something that stands for home and happiness that I wouldn't approach without a geiger counter and a bomb squad. It's okay. You eat yours and I'll eat mine. We could do worse.

Now everybody has some secret goals in life. And I've kind of been keeping my eye out for the ultimate chicken-fried-steak experience. You have to look in truck stops and little country towns off the freeway. Little temples of the holy meal out there in the underbrush.

If you're interested, this summer's search produced these results:

- One Star to the Torres Bar and Grill in Weiser, Idaho—free toothpicks, too.
- Two Stars to the Farewell Bend Cafe in Farewell Bend, Oregon—with special praise for a side of "Graveyard Stew," which is milk toast, and that's another story.
- Two Stars to the Blue Bucket in Umatilla, Oregon—free mints afterward.
- Three Stars to the Roostertail Truck Stop on Sixth Avenue South in Seattle—the waitress used to drive a truck in Alabama, and she knows all about chicken-fried steak.

FIVE STARS and a bouquet to Maud Owens' Cafe in Payette, Idaho, where the chicken-fried steak hangs over the edge of the plate and is accompanied by parsley, a spiced peach, two dill pickles, and a fried egg. *And* free toothpicks *AND* free mints. *And* a map of Payette under the plate.

The manager shook my hand when I left Maud Owens' Cafe. The waitress gave me a kiss on the cheek. I left her a two-dollar tip. I don't think anybody had ever eaten the whole thing before. I could still taste it three days later.

Now I suppose you are wondering why on earth I am telling all this. Well, I get tired of hearing it's a crummy world and that people are no damned good. What kind of talk is that? I know a place in Payette, Idaho, where a cook and a waitress and a manager put everything they've got into laying a chicken-fried steak on you.

The Rolling Stones are famous for their phrase about how you can't always get what you want but sometimes you can get what you need. Well, I'm here to tell you that sometimes you can get what you want *and* what you need at the same time, with free toothpicks and mints, and a kiss for topping!

IN THE EARLY DRY DARK of an October's Saturday evening, the neighborhood children are playing hide-and-seek. How long since I played hide-and-seek? Thirty years; maybe more. I remember how. I could become part of the game in a moment, if invited. Adults don't play hide-and-seek. Not for fun, anyway. Too bad.

Did you have a kid in your neighborhood who always hid so good, nobody could find him? We did. After a while we would give up on him and go off, leaving him to rot wherever he was. Sooner or later he would show up, all mad because we didn't keep looking for him. And we would get mad back because he wasn't playing the game the way it was supposed to be played. There's *hiding* and there's *finding*, we'd say. And he'd say it was hide-and-seek, not hide-and-give-UP, and we'd all yell about who made the rules and who cared about who, anyway, and how we wouldn't play with him anymore if he didn't get it straight and who needed him anyhow, and things like that. Hide-and-seek-and-yell. No matter what, though, the next time he would hide too good again. He's probably still hidden somewhere, for all I know.

As I write this, the neighborhood game goes on, and there is a kid under a pile of leaves in the yard just under my window. He has been there a long time now, and everybody else is found and they are about to give up on him over at the base. I considered going out to the base and telling them where he is hiding. And I thought about setting the leaves on fire to drive him out. Finally, I just yelled, "GET FOUND, KID!" out the window. And scared him so bad he probably wet his pants and started crying and ran home to tell his mother. It's real hard to know how to be helpful sometimes.

A man I know found out last year he had terminal cancer. He was a doctor. And knew about dying, and he didn't want to make his family and friends suffer through that with him. So he kept his secret. And died. Everybody said how brave he was to bear his suffering in silence and not tell everybody, and so on and so forth. But privately his family and friends said how angry they were that he didn't need them, didn't trust their strength. And it hurt that he didn't say good-bye.

He hid too well. Getting found would have kept him in the game. Hide-and-seek, grown-up style. Wanting to hide. Needing to be sought. Confused about being found. "I don't want anyone to know." "What will people think?" "I don't want to bother anyone."

Better than hide-and-seek, I like the game called Sardines. In Sardines the person who is It goes and hides, and everybody goes looking for him. When you find him, you get in with him and hide there with him. Pretty soon everybody is hiding together, all stacked in a small space like puppies in a pile. And pretty soon somebody giggles and somebody laughs and everybody gets found.

Medieval theologians even described God in hide-and-seek terms, calling him *Deus Absconditus*. But me, I think old God is a Sardine player. And will be found the same way everybody gets found in Sardines—by the sound of laughter of those heaped together at the end.

"Olly-olly-oxen-free." The kids out in the street are hollering the cry that says "Come on in, wherever you are. It's a new game." And so say I. To all those who have hid too good. *Get found, kid!* Olly-olly-oxen-free.

*H*OW ABOUT SOME GOOD NEWS for a change? Something to consider when you are in a people-are-no-damn-good mood?

Here's a phrase we hear a lot: "You can't trust anybody anymore." Doctors and politicians and merchants and salesmen. They're all out to rip you off, right?

It ain't necessarily so.

Man named Steven Brill tested the theory. In New York City, with taxicab drivers. Brill posed as a well-to-do foreigner with little knowledge of English. He got into several dozen taxis around New York City to see how many drivers would cheat him. His friends predicted in advance that most would take advantage of him in some way.

One driver out of thirty-seven cheated him. The rest took him directly to his destination and charged him correctly. Several refused to take him when his destination was only a block or two away, even getting out of their cabs to show him how close he already was. The greatest irony of all was that several drivers warned him that New York City was full of crooks and to be careful.

You will continue to read stories of crookedness and corruption—of policemen who lie and steal, doctors who reap where they do not sew, politicians on the take. Don't be misled. They are news because they are the exceptions. The evidence suggests that you can trust a lot more people than you think. The evidence suggests that a lot of people believe that. A recent survey by Gallup indicates that 70 percent of the people believe that most people can be trusted most of the time.

Who says people are no damn good? What kind of talk is that?

TRANSPORTATION IS MUCH THE TOPIC OF THE DAY. You've noticed. Our devotion to the car is worshipful. Eric Berne called it the cocktail-party pastime game, "General Motors."

Despite what you hear, it's not really a matter of economics. It's an image issue. In America, you are what you drive. Go out in the garage and look. There you are.

Well, my old hoopy has joined the cripples on the edge of the herd. And a new vehicle (image) is in order.

The silver-gray Mercedes with glove-leather everything really felt like me. The bank did not really think it felt like me to them. The shiny black BMW motorcycle with sidecar kind of felt like me. My wife did not think it felt like her—especially the sidecar part. The Land Rover with gun rack and shooting top felt like me. But there are so few game-covered veldts around town now. The VW Rabbit is *Consumer Reports'* choice, but a Rabbit I am just not. If they had named it the VW Walrus or the VW Water Buffalo, I might go for it. The Chrysler Coupe de Coupes de Coupes won't do, either. Who wants to be an anachronism?

One of my students suggested putting all my money into drugs. Stay home and take all the trips you want. But that's not me—you don't bring back groceries from those trips.

It's clear that what would be fashionably hip is a fine piece of engineering—something that's luxurious yet practical, useful, and economical. Like a Porsche pick-up truck that runs on Kleenex. Silver-gray, of course.

What I really want from transportation is not an image but a feeling.

I remember riding home on a summer's eve in the back of an ancient Ford pickup truck, with two eight-year-old cousins for company and my uncle Roscoe at the wheel. We'd been swimming and were sitting on the inner tubes for comfort, and had a couple of old quilts and an elderly dog wrapped close for warmth. We were eating chocolate cookies and drinking sweet milk out of a Mason jar, and singing our lungs out with unending verses of "Ninety-nine Bottles of Beer on the Wall." With stars and moon and God o'erhead, and sweet dreams at the end of the journey home.

Now *that's* transportation. The way I like to travel. And that's me. If you hear of a dealer, let me know.

FOR A TIME I LIVED on a steep hillside in a decrepit summer cottage that had what a real estate agent called "charm." Which meant it was a shack with a view.

In keeping with the spirit of the house, I let the yard go "natural," letting what wanted to be there *be* there and take care of itself without any help from me. I remember announcing from the front porch to all living things in the yard: "You're all on your own. Good luck."

Up the hill above me lived Mr. Washington. In a sleek, ranch-style brick-and-shingle dwelling with a yard kept like a combination golf course and arboretum. It was his pride and joy.

An older man, insurance agent, and a mighty cooking champion when it came to barbecued ribs and brisket, Mr. Washington was also Black. And I am not (I'm more putty-colored, actually).

It was the late sixties, and I was into civil rights and

being obsessively liberal about anything you cared to mention. Mr. Washington was into—well, I'll use his *exact* words: "Fulghum, you are a downwardly mobile honky, and I am an upwardly mobile nigger, and don't you forget it!" Then he'd laugh and laugh.

It made me nervous when he used that word. I didn't mind "honky," but that *other* word. But that's what he called himself, and he always laughed when he said it.

Mr. Washington looked down from his porch onto my ratty residence with amused contempt. He said he put up with me because I could cook better chili than he could and I had the best collection of power tools in the neighborhood.

Sometimes we played poker, and we shared both a fondness for fine cigars and the fact of wives who did not. We walked in the same marches of the times— the ones about justice and war. And we liked the same music, once spending most of an evening comparing the solos of John Coltrane and Johnny Hodges.

Always there was his laughter—no matter how grim or serious the world might get, he saw the comic strip we were all in.

In an uncommon way we provided a reference point for one another as we sorted out our daily lives, as you will see.

He's dead now. I really miss him. I still have his laughter in my mind, and I hear it at hard times.

And best of all, I have the recipe for his barbecue sauce.

MR. WASHINGTON WAS A HARD-CORE LAWN freak. His yard and my yard blended together in an ambiguous fashion. Every year he was seized by a kind of herbicidal mania. He started fondling his weed-eater and mixing up vile potions in vats in his garage. It usually added up to trouble.

Sure enough, one morning I caught him over in my yard spraying dandelions. "Didn't really think you'd mind," says he, righteously.

"Mind, *mind*!—you just killed my flowers," says I, with guarded contempt.

"Flowers?" he ripostes. "*Those* are *weeds*!" He points at my dandelions with utter disdain.

"Weeds," says I, "are plants growing where people don't want them. In other words," says I, "weeds are in the eye of the beholder. And as far as I am concerned, dandelions are not *weeds*—they are *flowers*!"

"Horse manure," says he, and stomps off home to avoid any taint of lunacy.

Now I happen to like dandelions a lot. They cover my yard each spring with fine yellow flowers, with no help from me at all. They mind their business and I mind mine. The young leaves make a spicy salad. The flowers add fine flavor and elegant color to a classic light wine. Toast the roots, grind and brew, and you have a palatable coffee. The tenderest shoots make a tonic tea. The dried mature leaves are high in iron, vitamins A and C, and make a good laxative. Bees favor dandelions, and the cooperative result is high-class honey.

Dandelions have been around for about thirty million years; there are fossils. The nearest relatives are lettuce and chicory. Formally classed as perennial herbs of the genus *Taraxacum* of the family *asteraceae*. The name comes from the French for lion's tooth, *dent de lion*. Distributed all over Europe, Asia, and North America, they got there on their own. Resistant to disease, bugs, heat, cold, wind, rain, and human beings.

If dandelions were rare and fragile, people would knock themselves out to pay $14.95 a plant, raise them by hand in greenhouses, and form dandelion societies and all that. But they are everywhere and don't need us and kind of do what they please. So we call them "weeds," and murder them at every opportunity.

Well, I say they are *flowers*, by God, and pretty

damn fine flowers at that. And I am *honored* to have them in my yard, where I *want* them. Besides, in addition to every other good thing about them, they are magic. When the flower turns to seed, you can blow them off the stem, and if you blow just right and all those little helicopters fly away, you get your wish. Magic. Or if you are a lover, they twine nicely into a wreath for your friend's hair.

I defy my neighbor to show me anything in his yard that compares with dandelions.

And if all that isn't enough, consider this: Dandelions are free. Nobody ever complains about your picking them. You can have all you can carry away. Some weed!

THE MAN NEXT DOOR CLEANED HIS GUTTERS yesterday. Downspouts too. He's done it before. I saw him last year. Amazing. I was forty years old before I even knew that people cleaned gutters and downspouts. And I haven't been able to get around to doing it once yet.

I live in awe of people who get those jobs done. The people who live orderly lives. The ones who always do what needs to be done and do it right. I know of people who actually balance their checkbooks each month. I know that's hardly credible, but I swear it's so.

These people also have filing cabinets (*not shoe boxes*) with neat, up-to-date, relevant files. They can find things around the house when they need them. There is order under their sinks, in their closets, and in the trunks of their cars. They actually change the filter on their furnace once a year. They put oil and grease on mechanical things. Their warranties runneth not out. Not only do their flashlights work, they actually *know* where the flashlights *are*!

When their car was last serviced—they know that too. The tools in their garage are on the pegboard—right where they are supposed to be. Their taxes are based on facts, not hunches and prayer. When they go to sleep at night, their list of Things to Do has a line through every item. And when they arise in the morning, their bathrobe is right there beside the bed and it is clean and new. Socks—right there in the drawer, folded into matching pairs. Yes! And as they prepare to walk out the door into a new day, they know exactly where their car keys are and are not worried about the state of the car battery or if there is enough gas to get to work.

There *are* such people. Ones who have it all together. Exempt from the reign of Chaos and the laws of entropy. I see them every day all around me. Calm and easy pillars of society. They are the people in your high school yearbook you wanted to be. The ones who made it.

Well. I am not one of them. Out of the frying pan, into the spilt milk is more me. Most of the time daily life is a lot like an endless chore of chasing chickens in a large pen. Life as an air-raid drill. Never mind the details.

But I have a recurring fantasy that sees me through.

It is my stick-polishing fantasy. One day a committee of elders will come to my door and tell me it is time to perform the ritual of the polished stick—a rite of passage for the good-at-heart-but-chronically-disorganized.

Here's the way it works. You get selected for this deal because you are such a good person at heart, and it is time you were let off the hook. First, a week of your life is given to you free of all obligations. Your calendar is wiped clean. No committee meetings, no overdue anything—bills, correspondence, or unanswered telephone calls. You are taken to a nice place, where it is all quiet and serene and Zen. You are cared for. Fed well. And often affirmed. Your task is simply this: to spend a week polishing a stick. They give you some sandpaper and lemon oil and rags. And, of course, the stick—a nice but ordinary piece of wood. All you have to do is polish it. As well as you can. Whenever you feel like it. That's it: *polish the stick*.

At the end of the week the elders will return. They will gravely examine your work. They will praise you for your expertise, your sensitivity, and your spiritual insight. "No stick was ever polished quite like *this*!" they will exclaim. Your picture will appear on TV and in the papers. The story will say, "Man who is good at heart and well intentioned has thoroughly and completely and admirably polished his stick!" You will be escorted home in quiet triumph.

Your family and neighbors will give you looks of respect. As you pass in the streets, people will smile knowingly and wave and give you a thumbs-up sign. You will have passed into another stage of being.

But more than that. From this time forward, you may ignore your gutters and downspouts. Your checkbook and files and forms and closets and drawers and taxes and even the trunk of your car will be taken care of for you. You are now exempt from these concerns. You are forever released from the bond of Things to Do. For you have *polished the stick*! Look at it hanging there over your mantel. Be proud, stick polisher! This is really something. And, it is enough.

Oh, don't I wish.

MAN NEXT DOOR AND I LOOK upon one another with suspicion. He's a raker and a shoveler, as I see it. A troubler of the natural ways of the earth. Left over from the breed that conquered the wilderness. He thinks of me in simpler terms: lazy.

See, every week during the fall he's out raking little leaves into little piles. And every time it snows, he's out tormenting the white stuff with his shovel. Once, out of either eagerness or outrage, he even managed to shovel a heavy frost. "Can't let old Mother Nature get ahead of you," says he.

So I tell him he hasn't the sense God gave a stump. In a kind of careful way. Leaves have been falling down for thousands and thousands of years, I tell him. And the earth did pretty well before rakes and people, I tell him. Old Mother Nature put the leaves where she wanted them and they made more earth. We need more earth, I tell him. We're running out of it, I tell him. And snow—snow is not my enemy, I tell him. Snow is God's way of telling people to slow down and rest and stay in bed for a day. And besides, snow always solves itself. Mixes with the leaves to form more earth, I tell him.

His yard *does* look neat, I must admit—*if* neatness is important. And he didn't fall down getting to his car last snowtime, and I in fact did. And he is a good neighbor, even if he is a raker and a shoveler. I'm open-minded about this thing.

Still, my yard has an Oriental carpet of red and yellow and green and brown. And his doesn't. And I spent the same time he spent shoveling snow collecting it in bottles to mix with orange juice July next, and I taped the sound of it falling and then used the tape to wrap Christmas presents (*snow has lots of uses*).

I gave him a bottle of vintage winter snow for Christmas, wrapped in some of that tape. He gave me a rake. We're giving each other lessons in the proper use of these tools. I think he's got no religion, and I'm trying to convert him. He thinks I've got too much, and he's trying to get me to back off.

But in the end, in the end, in the final end of it all— I win. For he and I—and even you—will become what the leaves and snow become, and go where the leaves and snow go—whether we rake or shovel or not.

*I*F YOU ASK MY NEXT-DOOR NEIGHBOR WHAT HE does for a living, he will tell you that he is a professional gambler involved in organized crime. In truth, he is an insurance agent. He has a healthy disrespect for his business, and extends that skeptical mode into his philosophy of life. "We're *all* gamblers," says he, "every one of us. And life is a continual crapshoot and poker game and horse race." Then he adds, "And I *love* the game!"

He's a great believer in hedging his bets, however, protecting himself by betting both ways when the odds are close. Philosophically this gets expressed in these sayings mounted on his office wall:

Always trust your fellow man. And always cut the cards.

Always trust God. And always build your house on high ground.

Always love thy neighbor. And always pick a good neighborhood to live in.

The race is not always to the swift, nor the battle to the strong, but you better bet that way.

Place your bet somewhere between turning-the-other-cheek and enough-is-enough-already.

Place your bet somewhere between haste-makes-waste and he-who-hesitates-is-lost.

About winning: It isn't important. What really counts is how you play the game.

About losing: It isn't important. What really counts is how you play the game.

About playing the game: Play to *win*!

Does he really believe that? Does he live by it? I don't know. But I play poker with him. And I bought my insurance from him. I like his kind of odds.

HAIR GROWS AT THE RATE of about half an inch a month. I don't know where he got his facts, but Mr. Washington came up with that one when we were comparing barbers. That means that about eight feet of hair had been cut off my head and face in the last sixteen years by my barber.

I hadn't thought much about it until I called to make my usual appointment and found that my barber had left to go into building maintenance. What? How could he *do* this? *My* barber. It felt like a death in the family. There was so much more to our relationship than sartorial statistics.

We started out as categories to each other: "barber" and "customer." Then we become "redneck ignorant barber" and "pinko egghead minister." Once a month we reviewed the world and our lives and explored our positions. We sparred over civil rights and Vietnam and a lot of elections. We became mirrors, confidants, confessors, therapists, and companions in an odd sort of way. We went through being thirty years old and then forty. We discussed and argued and joked, but always with a certain thoughtful deference. After all, I was his customer. And he was standing there with a razor in his hand.

I found out that his dad was a country policeman, that he grew up poor in a tiny town and had prejudices about Indians. He found out that I had the same small-town roots and grew up with prejudices about Blacks. Our kids were the same ages, and we suffered through the same stages of parenthood together. We shared wife stories and children stories and car troubles and lawn problems. I found out he gave his day off to giving free haircuts to old men in nursing homes. He found out a few good things about me, too, I suppose.

I never saw him outside the barber shop, never met his wife or children, never sat in his home or ate a meal with him. Yet he became a terribly important fixture in my life. Perhaps a lot more important than if we had been next-door neighbors. The quality of our relationship was partly created by a peculiar distance. There's a real sense of loss in his leaving. I feel like not having my hair cut anymore, though eight feet of hair might seem strange.

Without realizing it, we fill important places in each other's lives. It's that way with a minister and congregation. Or with the guy at the corner grocery, the mechanic at the local garage, the family doctor, teachers, neighbors, co-workers. Good people, who are always "there," who can be relied upon in small, important ways. People who teach us, bless us, encourage us, support us, uplift us in the dailiness of life. We never tell them. I don't know why, but we don't.

And, of course, we fill that role ourselves. There are those who depend on us, watch us, learn from us, take from us. And we never know. Don't sell yourself short. You may never have proof of your importance, but you are more important than you think.

It reminds me of an old Sufi story of a good man who was granted one wish by God. The man said he would like to go about doing good without knowing about it. God granted his wish. And then God decided that it was such a good idea, he would grant that wish to all human beings. And so it has been to this day.

G IANTS, WIZARDS, AND DWARFS was the game to play.

Being left in charge of about eighty children seven to ten years old, while their parents were off doing parenty things, I mustered my troops in the church social hall and explained the game. It's a large-scale version of Rock, Paper, and Scissors, and involves some intellectual decision making. But the real purpose of the game is to make a lot of noise and run around chasing people until nobody knows which side you are on or who won.

Organizing a roomful of wired-up gradeschoolers into two teams, explaining the rudiments of the game, achieving consensus on group identity—all this is no mean accomplishment, but we did it with a right good will and were ready to go.

The excitement of the chase had reached a critical mass. I yelled out: "You have to decide *now* which you are—a GIANT, a WIZARD, or a DWARF!"

While the groups huddled in frenzied, whispered consultation, a tug came at my pants leg. A small child stands there looking up, and asks in a small, concerned voice, "Where do the Mermaids stand?"

Where do the Mermaids stand?

A long pause. A *very* long pause. "Where do the Mermaids stand?" says I.

"Yes. You see, I am a Mermaid."

"There are no such things as Mermaids."

"Oh, yes, I am one!"

She did not relate to being a Giant, a Wizard, or a Dwarf. She knew her category. Mermaid. And was not about to leave the game and go over and stand against the wall where a loser would stand. She intended to participate, wherever Mermaids fit into the scheme of things. Without giving up dignity or identity. She took it for granted that there was a place for Mermaids and that I would know just where.

Well, where DO the Mermaids stand? All the "Mermaids"—all those who are different, who do not fit the norm and who do not accept the available boxes and pigeonholes?

Answer that question and you can build a school, a nation, or a world on it.

What was my answer at the moment? Every once in a while I say the right thing. "The Mermaid stands right here by the King of the Sea!" says I. (*Yes, right here by the King's Fool, I thought to myself.*)

So we stood there hand in hand, reviewing the troops of Wizards and Giants and Dwarfs as they roiled by in wild disarray.

It is not true, by the way, that mermaids do not exist. I know at least one personally. I have held her hand.

ONE YEAR I DIDN'T RECEIVE MANY Christmas cards. One fetid February afternoon this troublemaking realization actually came to me out of the back room in my head that is the source of useless information. Guess I needed some reason to really feel crummy, so there it was. But I didn't say anything about it. I can take it. I am tough. I won't complain when my cheap friends don't even care enough to send me a stupid Christmas card. I can do without love. Right.

The following August, I was nesting in the attic, trying to establish some order in the mess, and found stacked in with the holiday decorations a whole box of unopened greeting cards from the previous Christmas. I had tossed them into the box to open at leisure, and then I ran out of leisure in the shambles of the usual Christmas panic, so they got caught up in the bale-it-up-and-stuff-it-in-the-attic-and-we'll-straighten-it-out-next-year syndrome.

I hauled the box down, and on a hot summer day, middle of August, mind you, in my bathing suit, sitting in a lawn chair on my deck, with sunglasses, cocoa butter, a quart of iced tea, and a puzzled frame of mind, I began to open my Christmas cards. Just to help, I had put a tape of Christmas carols on the portable stereo and cranked up the volume.

Here it all was. Angels, snow, Wise Men, candles and pine boughs, horses and sleighs, the Holy Family, elves and Santa. Heavy messages about love and joy and peace and goodwill. If that wasn't enough, there were all those handwritten messages of affection from my cheap friends who had, in fact, come through for the holidays.

I cried. Seldom have I felt so bad and so good at the same time. So wonderfully rotten, elegantly sad, and melancholy and nostalgic and all. Bathos. Utter bathos.

As fate always seems to have it, I was discovered in this condition by a neighbor, who had been attracted to the scene by the sound of Christmas caroling. She laughed. I showed her the cards. She cried. And we had this outrageous Christmas ordeal right there on my deck in the middle of August, singing along with the Mormon Tabernacle Choir to the final mighty strains of "O Holy Night." "Faaallll on your kneeees, O heeeeeer the angel vooiiicees."

What can I say? I guess wonder and awe and joy are always there in the attic of one's mind somewhere, and it doesn't take a lot to set it off. And much about Christmas *is* outrageous, whether it comes to you in December or late August.

A SUNDAY AFTERNOON IT WAS, some days before Christmas. With rain, with wind, with cold. Wintersgloom. Things-to-do list was long and growing like an unresistant mold. Temper: short. Bio-index: negative. Horoscope reading suggested caution. And the Sunday paper suggested dollars, death, and destruction as the day's litany. O tidings of comfort and joy, fa la la la la!

This holy hour of Lordsdaybliss was jarred by a pounding at the door. Now what? Deep sigh. Opening it, resigned to accept whatever bad news lies in wait, I am nonplussed. A rather small person in a cheap Santa Claus mask, carrying a large brown paper bag outthrust: "TRICK OR TREAT!" Santa Mask shouts. What? "TRICK OR TREAT!" Santa Mask hoots again. Tongue-tied, I stare at this apparition. He shakes the bag at me, and dumbly I fish out my wallet and find a dollar to drop into the bag. The mask lifts, and it is an Asian kid with a ten-dollar grin taking up most of his face. "Wanta hear some caroling?" he asks, in singsong English.

I know him now. He belongs to a family settled into the neighborhood by the Quakers last year. Boat people. Vietnamese, I believe. Refugees. He stopped by at Halloween with his sisters and brothers, and I filled their bags. Hong Duc is his name—he's maybe eight. At Halloween he looked like a Wise Man, with a bathrobe on and a dish towel around his head.

"Wanta hear some caroling?"

I nod, envisioning an octet of urchin refugees hiding in the bushes ready to join their leader in uplifted song. "Sure, where's the choir?"

"I'm it," says he. And he launched forth with an up-tempo chorus of "Jingle Bells," at full lung power. This was followed by an equally enthusiastic rendering of what I swear sounded like "Hark, the Hairy Angels Sing." And finally, a soft-voiced, reverential singing of "Silent Night." Head back, eyes closed, from the bottom of his heart he poured out the last strains of "Sleep in heavenly peace" into the gathering night.

Wet-eyed, dumbstruck by his performance, I pulled a five-dollar bill out of my wallet and dropped that into the paper bag. In return he produced half a candy cane from his pocket and passed it solemnly to me. Flashing the ten-dollar grin, he turned and ran

from the porch, shouted "GOD BLESS YOU," and
"TRICK OR TREAT" and was gone.

Who was that masked kid? Hong Duc, the one-man
choir, delivering Christmas door to door.

I confess that I'm usually a little confused about
Christmas. It never has made a lot of sense to me. It's
unreal. Ever since I got the word about Santa Claus,
I've been a closet cynic at heart. Singing about riding
in a one-horse open sleigh is ludicrous. I've never seen
one, much less ridden in one. Never roasted chestnuts
by an open fire. Wouldn't know how to if I had one,
and I hear they're no big deal anyway. Wandering
Wise Men raise my suspicions, and shepherds who
spend their lives hanging about with sheep are a little
strange. Never seen an angel, either, and my experience with virgins is really limited. The appearance of
a newborn king doesn't interest me; I'd just as soon
settle for some other president. Babies and reindeer
stink. I've been around them both, and I know. The
little town of Bethlehem is a pit, according to those
who have been there.

Singing about things I've never seen or done or
wanted, dreaming of a white Christmas I've never
known. Christmas isn't very real. And yet, and yet
. . . I'm too old to believe in it, and too young to give
up on it. Too cynical to get into it, and too needy to
stay out of it.

Trick or treat! After I shut the door came near

hysteria—laughter and tears and that funny feeling you get when you know that once again Christmas has come to you. Right down the chimney of my midwinter hovel comes Saint Hong Duc. He is confused about the details, like me, but he is very clear about the spirit of the season. It's an excuse to let go and celebrate—to throw yourself into Holiday with all you have, wherever you are. "I'm it," says he. Where's Christmas? I ask myself. I'm it, comes the echo. I'm it. Head back, eyes closed, voice raised in whatever song I can muster the courage to sing.

God, it is said, once sent a child upon a starry night, that the world might know hope and joy. I am not sure that I quite believe that, or that I believe in all the baggage heaped upon that story during two thousand years. But I am sure that I believe in Hong Duc, the one-man Christmas choir, shouting "trick or treat!" door to door. I don't know who or what sent him. But I know I am tricked through the whimsical mischief of fate into joining the choir that sings of joy and hope. Through a child, I have been treated to Christmas.

AND SPEAKING OF GIFTS, I SHOULD tell you a rule. It is not my rule, necessarily. It came from a very grumpy-looking man at a holiday office party. A man coming down with a full-blown case of Scrooge-itis. He had just unwrapped his dinky little present from under the office tree. In tones of amused sorrow he said to nobody in particular:

"You know, it's not true that what counts is the thought and not the gift. It just isn't true. My mother was pulling my leg on that one. I have collected so much gift-wrapped trash over the years from people who copped out and hurriedly bought a little plastic cheapie to give under the protective flag of good *thoughts*. I tell you, it is the *gift* that counts. Or, rather, people who think good *thoughts* give good *gifts*. It ought to be a rule—the *Brass Rule* of *Gift Exchange*."

And he stomped off toward a garbage can carrying his little gift as if it were a dead roach.

Well, maybe so. It's a kind of harsh judgment, and a little close for comfort. But the spirit of the season has been clear for a long time. God, who, it is said, started all this, cared enough to send the very best. On more than one occasion. And the Wise Men did not come bearing tacky knickknacks. Even old Santa, when he's making his list, is checking it twice. And the Angels came bringing Good News, which was not about a half-price sale.

I DO KNOW WHAT I WANT someone to give me for Christmas. I've known since I was forty years old. Wind-up mechanical toys that make noises and go round and round and do funny things. No batteries. Toys that need me to help them out from time to time. The old-fashioned painted tin ones I had as a child. That's what I want. Nobody believes me. It's what I want, I tell you.

Well, okay, that's close, but not quite exactly it. It's delight and simplicity that I want. Foolishness and fantasy and noise. Angels and miracles and wonder and innocence and magic. That's closer to what I want.

It's harder to talk about, but what I *really*, *really*, *really* want for Christmas is just this:

I want to be five years old again for an hour.

I want to laugh a lot and cry a lot.

I want to be picked up and rocked to sleep in someone's arms, and carried up to bed just one more time.

I know what I really want for Christmas.

I want my childhood back.

Nobody is going to give me that. I might give at least the memory of it to myself if I try. I know it doesn't make sense, but since when is Christmas about sense, anyway? It is about a child, of long ago and far away, and it is about the child of now. In you and me. Waiting behind the door of our hearts for something wonderful to happen. A child who is impractical, unrealistic, simpleminded, and terribly vulnerable to joy. A child who does not need or want or understand gifts of socks or potholders.

The Brass Rule is true.

*A*LWAYS WANTED A CUCKOO CLOCK. A big baroque German job with all kinds of carved foobaz and a little bird that leaps out once an hour and hollers an existential comment about life. So I got one. For my best friend, who also happens to be my wife and lives in the same house with me. See, the way this deal works is that she usually doesn't really like what I give her for Christmas, anyway, and I usually end up with it in the end, so I figured I might as well start out by giving her something I want in the first place, so when I get it back I can be truly grateful. She gets the thought; I get the gift. I know it's wicked, but it's realistic and practical. *(And don't get high-minded about this, as if you would never think of doing such a thing. The hell you say. I've been around. I know what I know.)*

Anyway, I wanted an authentic antique cuckoo clock. But they cost a bundle. And this store had new ones—overstocked—a special cheap price—hot deal.

So I bought one. There were two messages written in small print on the carton, which I missed reading. "Made in South Korea" was one. And "Some Assembly Is Required" was the other.

The carton produced five plastic bags of miscellaneous parts. And an ersatz Bavarian alpine goatherd hut marked "genuine simulated wood." And to top it off, a plastic deer head that looked like Bambi's mother. I put it all together with no parts left over, thank you, and hung it on the wall. Pulled down the weights, pushed the pendulum, and stepped back. It ticked and tocked in a comforting kind of way. Never before had such an enterprise gone quite so well for me. The damned thing actually worked!

The hour struck. The little door opened. The little bird did not come out. But from deep in its little hole came a raspy, muffled "cukaa, cukaa, cukaa." Three "cukaas"? That's it? That's all? But the hands of the clock said noon.

I peered deep into the innards of the Bavarian alpine goatherd hut of simulated wood. There was the bird. Using an ice pick and a chopstick, I tried to pry the creature forth. It seemed loose. I reset the clock to three. The clock ticked and tocked and then clanged. The door was flung open. No bird. Out of the darkness at the back of the hut came "cuck" but no "oo"— not even "aa."

Applying the principle of "if it won't move, force

it," I resorted to a rubber mallet and a coat hanger, followed by a vigorous shaking. Reset the clock. Hour struck. Door opened. Silence.

Close inspection revealed a small corpse with a spring around its neck, lying on its side. Not many people have murdered a cuckoo-clock bird, but I had done it. I could see Christmas morning: "Here, dear, a cuckoo clock. For you. The bird is dead."

And I did. I gave her the clock. And I told her the story. And she laughed. She kept the clock, too, dead bird and all, for a while.

The clock and its bird are long gone from our house now. And Christmas has come and gone many times as well. But the story gets told every year when we gather with friends in December. They laugh. And my wife looks at me and grins her grin and I grin back. She reminds me that the real cuckoo bird in the deal was not the critter inside the clock. I remember.

And me. Well, I still don't have a cuckoo clock of my own. But I have kept something. It is the memory of the Christmas message written on the packing carton. It said, "Some Assembly Is Required." To assemble the best that is within you and give it away. And to assemble with those you love to rekindle joy. Cuckoo to you, old bird, and Merry Christmas, wherever you are.

FOLKS ACROSS THE STREET are really with-it types. They jog and scarf bean sprouts and recycle everything but the air they breathe. Liberation is a big thing with them, too. Both men's and women's. They aren't married—they have a "contract"—and lead independent lives. Their consciousness is so raised they float. Nice folks. Give the neighborhood a progressive tone. Well, so.

They bought themselves an 18-speed mountain bicycle. Tandem. On the grounds of economy and efficiency. They've been riding it every day. In matching cycle suits and leather helmets, with jugs of go-juice and everything. He always rides in front, I notice. He always steers. Always. Not very libby, really.

Conversations with each of them separately reveal the age-old truth. Privately, he thinks he's stronger and has a better sense of direction. She lets him.

Because she gets to look around and enjoy the scenery; because she can stop pedaling and he doesn't notice; and if they crash, he's good padding.

The everlasting tandem. Men in front, women to the rear. It's probably true that men are stronger. But women are smarter—at least this one is. Liberation, I guess, is everybody getting what they think they want, without knowing the whole truth. Or in other words, liberation finally amounts to being free from things we don't like in order to be enslaved by things we approve of. Here's to the eternal tandem.

THE RAP ON THE DOOR WAS SHARP, urgent, insistent—a foreboding of crisis—rappity-rappity-rappity *rap* . . . Me, rushing to the door, fumbling with the lock, pumping my adrenaline, preparing for emergency. Small boy. Odd expression. Hands me a scrawled note on much-folded paper: "My name is Donnie. I will rake your leaves. $1 a yard. I am deaf. You can write to me. I can read. I rake good."

(Across the back of our house is a row of middle-aged matronly maple trees, extravagantly dressed in season in a million leaf-sequins. And in season the sequins detach. Not much wind in our sheltered yard, so the leaves lie about the ladies' feet now like dressing gowns they've stepped out of in preparation for the bath of winter.

(I like the way it looks. I like the way it looks very much. My wife does not. The gardening magazine does not like it, either. Leaves should be raked. There are rules. Leaves are not good for grass. Leaves are untidy. Leaves are

moldyslimy. But I like leaves so much, I once filled my classroom at school ankle-deep with them.

(There is a reason for leaves. There is no reason for mowed grass. So say I.

(My wife does not see it this way. There is an unspoken accusation in the air of laziness. We have been through this before. But this year a bargain has been struck in the name of the Scientific Method. Half the yard will be properly raked, and the other half will be left in the care of nature. Come summer, we shall see. And so her part is raked and mine is not. Let it be.)

Like a pilot in a fog relying on limited instruments, the boy looks intently at my face for information. He knows I have leaves. He has seen them. Mine is the *only* yard in the neighborhood with leaves, in fact. He knows his price is right. Solemnly he holds out pencil and paper for my reply. How can I explain to him about the importance of the scientific experiment going on in my backyard?

(In a way, the trees are there because of the leaves. With unbridled extravagance, zillions of seeds have helicoptered out of the sky to land like assault forces to green the earth. The leaves follow to cover, protect, warm, and nourish the next generation of trees. Stony ground, rot, mold, bacteria, birds, squirrels, bugs, and people—all intervene. But somehow, some make it. Some tenacious seeds take hold and hold on and hold on—for dear life. In the silence of winter's dark they prevail and plant themselves and survive to become the

*next generation of trees. It has been thus for eons, and we
mess with the process at our peril, say I. This is important.)*

"My name is Donnie. I will rake your leaves. $1 a
yard. I am deaf. You can write to me. I can read. I
rake good." He holds out the pencil and paper with
patience and hope and goodwill.

There are times when the simplest of events call all
of one's existential motives into question. What
would I do if he wasn't deaf? What will it do for him
if I say no? If I say yes? What difference? We stand in
each other's long silence, inarticulate for different reasons. In the same motion, he turns to go and I reach
for the pencil and paper to write, solemnly: "Yes.
Yes, I would like to have my leaves raked." A grave
nod from the attentive businessmanchild. "Do you
do it when they are wet?"

"Yes," he writes.

"Do you have your own rake?"

"No."

"This is a big yard—there are lots of leaves."

"Yes."

"I think I should give you two dollars."

A smile. "Three?" he writes.

A grin.

We have a contract. The rake is produced, and
Donnie the deaf leaf-raker goes to work in the fast-
falling November twilight. In silence he rakes. In

silence I watch—through the window of the dark house. Are there any sounds at all in his mind? I wonder. Or only the hollow, empty sea-sound I get when I put my fingers in my ears as tightly as I can.

Carefully he rakes the leaves into a large pile, as instructed. *(Yes, I am thinking I will spread them out over the yard again after he is gone. I am stubborn about this.)* Carefully he goes back over the yard picking up missed leaves by hand and carrying them to the pile. He also is stubborn about *his* values. Raking leaves means *all* the leaves.

Signing that he must go because it is dark and he must go home to eat, he leaves the work unfinished. Having paid in advance, I wonder if he will return. At age forty-five, I am cynical. Too cynical. Come morning, he has returned to his task, first checking the previously raked yard for latecomers. He takes pride in his work. The yard is leaf-free. I note his picking up several of the brightest yellow leaves and putting them into the pocket of his sweat shirt. Along with a whole handful of helicoptered seeds.

Rappity-rappity-rappity-*rap*! He reports to the door, signing that the work is done. As he walks away up the street I see him tossing one helicoptered seed into the air at a time. Fringe benefits. I stand in my own door in my own silence, smiling at his grace. Fringe benefits.

Tomorrow I will go out and push the pile of leaves

over the bank into the compost heap at the bottom of the ravine behind our house. I will do it in silence. The leaves and seeds will have to work out their destiny there this year. I could not feel right about undoing his work. My experiment with science will have to stand aside for something more human. The leaves let go, the seeds let go, and I must let go sometimes, too, and cast my lot with another of nature's imperfect but tenacious survivors.

Hold on, Donnie, hold on.

TALKING WITH A NICE LADY ON THE PHONE. She
has a case of the midwinter spiritual rot. And a terminal cold she's had since September 1.

"Well," rasps she, "you don't ever get depressed,
do you?"

"Listen," says I, "I get lows it takes extension lad-
ders to get out of."

"So what do you do?" asks she. "I mean, what DO
YOU DO?"

Nobody ever pinned me down quite like that before. They usually ask what I think *they* should do.

My solace is not religion or yoga or rum or even
deep sleep. It's Beethoven. As in Ludwig van. He's
my ace in the hole. I put his Ninth Symphony on the
stereo, pull the earphones down tight, and lie down
on the floor. The music comes on like the first day of
Creation.

And I think about old Mr. B. He knew a whole lot

about depression and unhappiness. He moved around from place to place trying to find the right place. His was a lousy love life, and he quarreled with his friends all the time. A rotten nephew worried him deeply— a nephew he really loved. Mr. B. wanted to be a virtuoso pianist. He wanted to sing well, too. But when still quite young, he began to lose his hearing. Which is usually bad news for pianists and singers. By 1818, when he was forty-eight, he was stone-cold deaf. Which makes it all the more amazing that he finished his great Ninth Symphony five years later. He never really *heard* it! He just *thought* it!

So I lie there with my earphones on, wondering if it ever could have felt to Beethoven like it sounds in my head. The crescendo rises, and my sternum starts to vibrate. And by the time the final kettledrum drowns out all those big F's, I'm on my feet, singing at the top of my lungs in gibberish German with the mighty choir, and jumping up and down as the legendary Fulghumowski directs the final awesome moments of the END OF THE WORLD AND THE COMING OF GOD AND ALL HIS ANGELS, HALLELUJAH! HALLELUJAH! WWHHOOOO-OOOOM-KABOOM-BAM-BAAAAAA!!!   Lord!

Uplifted, exalted, excited, affirmed, and over-whelmed am I! MANALIVE! Out of all that sorrow and trouble, out of all that frustration and disappoint-ment, out of all that deep and permanent silence, came all that majesty—that outpouring of JOY and exaltation! He *defied* his fate with *jubilation*!

And I never can resist all that truth and beauty. I just can't manage to continue sitting around in my winter ash heap, wringing my hands and feeling sorry for myself, in the face of THAT MUSIC! Not only does it wipe out spiritual rot, it probably cures colds, too.

So what's all this noise about winter and rain and bills and taxes? says I to me. So who *needs* all this talk about failure and confusion and frustration? What's all this noise about life and people being no damned good?

In the midst of oatmeal days, I find within Beethoven's music an irresistible affirmation. In deep, spiritual winter, I find inside myself the sun of summer. And some day, some incredible December night when I am very rich, I am going to rent me a grand hall and a great choir and a mighty symphony orchestra, and stand on the podium and conduct the Ninth. And I will personally play the kettledrum part all the way through to the glorious end, while simultaneously singing along at the very top of my lungs. And in the awesome silence that follows, I will bless all-the-gods-that-be for Ludwig van Beethoven, for his Ninth, and his light.

MANALIVE!

THERE'S A CLAY TABLET in the British Museum that's dated about 3800 B.C.—Babylonian. It's a census report—a people count—to determine tax revenues. The Egyptians and the Romans conducted census counts. And there's William the Conqueror's famous Domesday Book, compiled in England in 1085.

In our own country, the census dates from 1790. Soon we will do it again. Counting people tells some interesting things. Especially since computers enable us to extrapolate trends into the future. Take this, for example: If the population of the earth were to increase at the present rate indefinitely, by A.D. 3530 the total mass of human flesh and blood would equal the mass of the earth; and by A.D. 6826, the total mass of human flesh and blood would equal the mass of the known universe.

It boggles the mind, doesn't it?

Or consider this one: The total population of the earth at the time of Julius Caesar was 150 million. The total population *increase* in two years on earth today is 150 million.

Or bring it down into a smaller chunk: In the time it takes you to read this, about 200 people will die and about 480 people will be born. That's about two minutes' worth of life and death.

The statisticians figure that about 60 billion people have been born so far. And as I said, there's no telling how many more there will be, but it looks like a lot. And yet—and here comes the statistic of statistics—with all the possibilities for variation among the sex cells produced by each person's parents, it seems quite certain that each one of the billions of human beings who has ever existed has been distinctly different from every other human being, and that this will continue for the indefinite future.

In other words, if you were to line up on one side of the earth every human being who ever lived or ever will live, and you took a good look at the whole motley crowd, *you wouldn't find anybody quite like you*.

Now wait, there's more.

If you were to line up on the other side of the earth every *other* living thing that ever was or will be, you'd find that the creatures on the people side would be *more* like you than *anything* over on the other side.

Finally, this: There was a famous French criminologist named Emile Locard, and fifty years ago he came up with something called Locard's Exchange Principle. It says something to the effect that any person passing through a room will unknowingly deposit something there and take something away. Modern technology proves it. Fulghum's Exchange Principle extends it: Every person passing through this life will unknowingly leave something and take something away. Most of this "something" cannot be seen or heard or numbered. It does not show up in a census. But nothing counts without it.

*E*LIAS SCHWARTZ REPAIRS SHOES. He's short and round and bald and single and middle-aged and Jewish. "An old-fashioned cobbler," says he, nothing more, nothing less. I happen to be convinced that he is really the 145th reincarnation of the Haiho Lama.

See, the Haiho Lama died in 1937, and the monks of the Sa-skya monastery have been searching for forty years for his reincarnation without success. *The New York Times* carried the story last summer. The article noted that the Lama would be recognized by the fact that he went around saying and doing wise things in small, mysterious ways, and that he would be doing the will of God without understanding why.

Through some unimaginable error in the cosmic switching yards, the Haiho Lama has been reincarnated as Elias Schwartz. I have no doubts about it.

My first clue came when I took my old Bass loafers in for total renewal. The works. Elias Schwartz examined them with intense care. With regret in his voice he pronounced them not worthy of repair. I accepted the unwelcome judgment. Then he took my shoes, disappeared into the back of the shop, and I waited and wondered. He returned with my shoes in a stapled brown bag. For carrying, I thought.

When I opened the bag at home that evening, I found two gifts and a note. In each shoe, a chocolate-chip cookie wrapped in waxed paper. And these words in the note: "Anything not worth doing is worth not doing well. Think about it. Elias Schwartz."

The Haiho Lama strikes again.

And the monks will have to go on looking. Because I'll never tell—we need all the Lamas here we can get.

MOVING IS A BLOW TO MY SELF-IMAGE. I do like to think I am reasonably clean and tidy. But comes that moment after all the furniture and possessions have been removed from my rooms and I come back to see if I've left anything, and I look at the floor and there's all this STUFF around. Behind where the desk was and behind where the bookcase was and behind where the bed was and in the corner occupied by the chest.

Stuff. Gray, fuzzy, grotty Stuff.

Look at all that dirt, I think. I am not so very nice and clean after all, I think. What would the neighbors think? I think. What would my mother say? I think. What if *they* come to inspect? I think. I got to clean it up quick, I think. This Stuff. It's *always* there when I move. *What is it?*

I read in a medical journal that a laboratory analyzed this Stuff. They were working on the problems of people with allergies, but their results apply here.

The findings: particles of wool, cotton, and paper, bug chunks, food, plants, tree leaves, ash, microscopic spores of fungi and single-celled animals, and a lot of unidentifiable odds and ends, mostly natural and organic.

But that's just the miscellaneous list. The majority of Stuff comes from just two sources: *people*—exfoliated skin and hair; and *meteorites*—disintegrated as they hit the earth's atmosphere. *(No kidding—it's true—tons of it fall every day.)* So, in other words, what's behind my bed and bookcase and dresser and chest is mostly me and stardust.

A botanist told me that if you gather up a bunch of Stuff in a jar and put some water in it and let it sit in the sunlight and plant a seed in it, the seed will grow like crazy; or if you do the same thing but put it in a damp, dark place, mushrooms will grow in it. And then, if you eat the mushrooms, you see stars.

Also, if you really want to see a lot of it, take the sheet off your bed, shake it hard in a dark room, and then turn on a beamed flashlight. There you are. Like the little snowman in the round glass ball on the mantel at Grandma's house. London Bridge is falling down and I am falling down and the stars are falling down. And everything else is falling down, to go around again, some say.

Scientists have pretty well established that we come from a stellar birthing room. We are the Stuff of stars.

And there behind my desk, I seem to be returning to my source, in a quiet way. Recombining with the Stuff of the universe into who-knows-what. And I've a heightened respect for what's going on in the nooks and crannies of my very own room. It isn't dirt. It's cosmic compost.

ONE PORTION OF A MINISTER'S LOT concerns the dying and the dead. The hospital room, the mortuary, the funeral service, the cemetery. What I know of such things shapes my life elsewhere in particular ways. What I know of such things explains why I don't waste much life time mowing grass or washing cars or raking leaves or making beds or shining shoes or washing dishes. It explains why I don't honk at people who are slow to move at green lights. And why I don't kill spiders. There isn't time or need for all this. What I know of cemeteries and such also explains why I sometimes visit the Buffalo Tavern.

The Buffalo Tavern is, in essence, mongrel America. Boiled down and stuffed into the Buffalo on a Saturday night, the fundamental elements achieve a critical mass around eleven. The catalyst is the favorite house band, the Dynamic Volcanic Logs. Eight freaks frozen in the amber vibes of the sixties. Playing stomp-hell rockabilly with enough fervor to heal the lame and the halt. Mongrel America comes to the Buffalo to drink beer, shoot pool, and dance. Above all, to dance. To shake their tails and stomp frogs and get rowdy and holler and sweat and *dance*. When it's Saturday night and the Logs are rocking and the crowd is rolling, there's no such thing as death.

One such night the Buffalo was invaded by a motorcycle club, trying hard to look like the Hell's Angels and doing pretty good at it, too. I don't think these people were in costume for a movie. And neither they nor their ladies smelled like soap-and-water was an important part of their lives on anything like a daily basis. Following along behind them was an Indian—an older man, with braids, beaded vest, army surplus pants, and tennis shoes. He was really ugly. Now I'm fairly resourceful with words, and I would give you a flashy description of this man's face if it would help, but there's no way around it—he looked, in a word, ugly. He sat working on his Budweiser for a long time. When the Dynamic Logs ripped into a scream-out version of "Jailhouse Rock" he moved. Shuffled over to one of the motorcycle mommas and invited her to dance. Most ladies would have refused, but she was amused enough to shrug and get up.

Well, I'll not waste words. This ugly, shuffling Indian ruin could *dance*. I mean, he had the *moves*. Nothing wild, just effortless action, subtle rhythm, the cool of the master. He turned his partner every way but loose and made her look good at it. The floor slowly cleared for them. The band wound down and out, but the drummer held the beat. The motor-cycle-club group rose up and shouted for the band to keep playing. The band kept playing. The Indian kept dancing. The motorcycle momma finally blew a gasket and collapsed in someone's lap. The Indian danced on alone. The crowd clapped up the beat. The Indian danced with a chair. The crowd went crazy. The band faded. The crowd cheered. The Indian held up his hands for silence as if to make a speech. Looking at the band and then the crowd, the Indian said, "Well, what're you waiting for? Let's DANCE."

The band and the crowd went off like a bomb. People were dancing all through the tables to the back of the room and behind the bar. People were dancing in the restrooms and around the pool tables. Dancing for themselves, for the Indian, for God and Mammon. Dancing in the face of hospital rooms, mortuaries, funeral services, and cemeteries. And for a while, nobody died.

"Well," said the Indian, "what're you waiting for? Let's dance."

JUMPER CABLES? You got jumper cables, buddy?"
"Yeah, sure. I got jumper cables."

English teacher and his nice sweet wife, from Nampa, Idaho (as it turned out). In their funny little foreign car. Drove around town with their lights on in the morning fog and left the lights on, and so forth and so on. Dead meat now. Need jumper cables. Need battery. Need Good Samaritan. Need a friendly hand from someone who looks like he knows what to do with jumper cables. And the Good Fairy of Fate placed them in my hands.

Men are supposed to know about jumper cables. It's supposed to be in the genetic code, right? But some of us men are mental mutants, and if it's under the hood of a car, well it's voodoo, Jack, and that's the end of it.

Besides, this guy only asked me if I *had* jumper cables. He didn't ask me if I knew how to *use* them. I thought by the way he asked that he knew what he was doing. After all, he had an Idaho license plate and was wearing a baseball cap and cowboy boots. All *those* kind of people know about jumper cables when they're born, don't they? Guess he thought a white-bearded old man wearing hiking boots and driving a twenty-year-old VW van was bound to use jumper cables a lot. So I get out my cables, and we swagger around being all macho and cool and talking automobile talk. We look under the hood of his rig, and there's no battery.

"Hell," I said, "there's your problem right there. Somebody stole your battery."

"Dang," he said.

"The battery is under the backseat," said his nice sweet wife.

"Oh."

So we took all the luggage out of the backseat and hauled the seat out into the parking lot and, sure enough, there it was. A battery. Right there. Just asking for jumper cables to be laid on it. I began to get worried when the guy smirked at his wife and said under his breath that he took auto mechanics and sex education at the same time in high school and they had been confused in his mind ever since, when it came to where things were and what you did to get any action out of them. We laughed. His wife didn't laugh at all. She just pulled out a manual and started thumbing through it.

Anyway, the sum of our knowledge was that positive poles and negative poles were involved, and either one or both cars ought to be running, and six-volt and twelve-volt batteries and other-volt batteries did or did not work out. I thought he knew what he was doing, and kind of went along with it. Guess he did the same. And we hooked it all up real tight and turned the ignition key in both cars at the same time. And there was this electrical arc between the cars that not only fried his ignition system, it welded the jumper cables to my battery and knocked the baseball cap off his head. The sound was like that of the world's largest fly hitting one of those electric killer screens. *ZISH*. Accompanied by an *awesome* blue flash and some smoke. Power is an amazing thing.

We just sat down right there in the backseat of his car, which was still sitting out there in the parking lot. Awed by what we had accomplished. And his wife went off with the manual to find some semi-intelligent help. We talked as coolly and wisely as we could in the face of circumstances. He said, "Ignorance and power and pride are a deadly mixture, you know."

"Sure are," I said. "Like matches in the hands of a three-year-old. Or automobiles in the hands of a sixteen-year-old. Or faith in God in the mind of a saint or a maniac. Or a nuclear arsenal in the hands of a movie character. Or even jumper cables and batteries in the hands of fools." *(We were trying to get something cosmic and serious out of our own invocation of power, you see. Humbled as we were.)*

Some time later I got a present in the mail from Nampa, Idaho. From the guy's nice sweet wife. As a gesture of grace—forgiveness combined with instruction and admonition to go and sin no more. What she sent was a set of electronic true-start, foolproof, tangle-free jumper cables. Complete with instructions that tell you everything and more than you ever wanted to know about jumper cables, in English and Spanish. The set is designed so that when you get everything all hooked up, a little solid-state switch control box tells you if you've done it right or not, before any juice flows. Gives you time to *think* if you really want to go ahead with jumping the juice. We could all use a device like that between us and power, I guess. It's nice to know that progress in such things is possible—in the face of ignorance and pride. Progress is possible.

Jumper cables? You want jumper cables? Sure I got jumper cables. I can hook you up to Grand Coulee Dam, buddy. Or wire you into Almighty God. Or whatever powers there be. *Amen!*

THE FOURTH DAY OF THE MONTH OF JUNE, 1783—
more than two hundred years ago. The market square
of the French village of Annonay, not far from Paris.
On a raised platform, a smoky bonfire fed by wet
straw and old wool rags. Tethered above, straining at
its lines, a huge taffeta bag—a *balon*—thirty-three feet
in diameter.

In the presence of a "respectable assembly and a
great many other people," and accompanied by great
cheering, the *machine de l'aerostat* was cut from its
moorings and set free to rise majestically into the
noontide sky. Six thousand feet into the air it went,
and came to earth several miles away in a field, where
it was attacked by pitchfork-waving peasants and torn
to pieces as an instrument of evil. The first public
ascent of a balloon, the first step in the history of
human flight.

Old Ben Franklin was there, in France as the agent
of the new American states. He of the key and the kite

and the lightning and the bifocals and the printing press. When a bystander asked what possible good this *balon* thing could be, Franklin made the memorable retort: *"Eh, à quoi bon l'enfant qui vient de naître?"* ("What good is a newborn baby?") A man of such curiosity and imagination could provide an answer to his own question, and in his journal he wrote: "This *balon* will open the skies to mankind." The peasants, too, were not far from wrong. It was also a harbinger of great evil, in that Annonay would one day be leveled by bombs falling from the sky. But I am getting ahead of myself.

Some months before that June day, Joseph-Michel Montgolfier sat of an evening staring into his fireplace, watching sparks and smoke rise up the chimney from the evening fire. His imagination rose with the smoke. If smoke floated into the sky, why not capture it and put it in a bag and see if the bag would rise, perhaps carrying something or someone with it?

In his mid-forties, the son of a prosperous paper maker, a believer in the great church that was Science in the eighteenth century, a brilliant and impatient man with time on his hands was Monsieur Montgolfier. And so, with his younger, more methodical brother, Etienne, and the resources of their father's factory, he set to. With paper bags, then silken ones, and finally taffeta coated with resins. And *voilà*! Came a day when from the gardens at Versailles a balloon carrying a sheep, a rooster, and a duck went aloft. All survived, proving that there were no poisonous gases in the sky, as some had feared.

The most enthusiastic supporter of the brothers Montgolfier was a young chemist, Jean-François Pilâtre de Rozier. He didn't want to make balloons; he wanted to go up in one. The Montgolfier's interest was in scientific experimentation. They were older, wiser groundlings. Pilâtre wanted to *fly*. He was full of the adventure of youth. And so, that fall, November 21, 1783, Jean-François Pilâtre de Rozier got his wish. In the garden of the royal palace at La Muette, in the Bois de Boulogne, at 1:54 P.M., in a magnificent balloon seven stories high, painted with signs of the zodiac and the king's monogram. Up, up, and away he went— higher than treetops and church steeples—coming down beyond the Seine, five miles away.

Joseph-Michel and Etienne Montgolfier lived long and productive scientific lives, and died in their beds, safe on the ground. Two years after his historic flight, trying to cross the English Channel west to east in a balloon, the young Jean-François Pilâtre de Rozier plummeted from the sky in flames to his death. But his great-great grandson was later to become one of the first airplane pilots in France.

Well, what's all this about, anyway? It's about the power (and the price) of imagination. "Imagination is more important than information." Einstein said that, and he should know.

It's also a story about how people of imagination

stand on one another's shoulders. From the ground to the balloon to the man in the balloon to the man on the moon. Yes. Some of us are ground crew—holding lines, building fires, dreaming dreams, letting go, watching the upward flight. Others of us are bound for the sky and the far edges of things. That's in the story, too.

These things come to mind at the time of year when children graduate to the next stage of things. From high school, from college, from the nest of the parent. What shall we give them on these occasions? Imagination, a shove out and up, a blessing.

Come over here, we say—to the edge, we say. I want to show you something, we say. We are afraid, they say; it's very exciting, they say. Come to the edge, we say, use your imagination. And they come. And they look. And we push. And they fly. We to stay and die in our beds. They to go and to die howsoever, inspiring those who come after them to come to their own edge. And fly.

These things come to mind, too, in this middle year of my own life. I, too, intend to live a long and useful life and die safe in my bed on the ground. But the anniversary of that little event in the village of Annonay just happens to be my birthday. And on its bicentennial I went up in a balloon, from a field near the small Skagit Valley village of La Conner.

It's *never* too late to fly!

NOW LET ME TELL YOU ABOUT LARRY WALTERS, my hero. Walters is a truck driver, thirty-three years old. He is sitting in his lawn chair in his backyard, wishing he could fly. For as long as he could remember, he wanted to go *up*. To be able to just rise right up in the air and see for a long way. The time, money, education, and opportunity to be a pilot were not his. Hang gliding was too dangerous, and any good place for gliding was too far away. So he spent a lot of summer afternoons sitting in his backyard in his ordinary old aluminum lawn chair—the kind with the webbing and rivets. Just like the one you've got in your backyard.

The next chapter in this story is carried by the newspapers and television. There's old Larry Walters up in the air over Los Angeles. Flying at last. Really getting UP there. Still sitting in his aluminum lawn chair, but it's hooked on to forty-five helium-filled surplus weather balloons. Larry has a parachute on, a CB radio, a six-pack of beer, some peanut butter and jelly sandwiches, and a BB gun to pop some of the balloons to come down. And instead of being just a couple of hundred feet over his neighborhood, he shot up eleven thousand feet, right through the approach corridor to the Los Angeles International Airport.

Walters is a taciturn man. When asked by the press why he did it, he said: "You can't just sit there." When asked if he was scared, he answered: "Wonderfully so." When asked if he would do it again, he said: "Nope." And asked if he was glad that he did it, he grinned from ear to ear and said: "Oh, yes."

The human race sits in its chair. On the one hand is the message that says there's nothing left to do. And the Larry Walterses of the earth are busy tying balloons to their chairs, directed by dreams and imagination to do their thing.

The human race sits in its chair. On the one hand is the message that the human situation is hopeless. And the Larry Walterses of the earth soar upward knowing anything is possible, sending back the message from eleven thousand feet: "I did it, I really did it. I'm FLYING!"

It's the spirit here that counts. The time may be long, the vehicle may be strange or unexpected. But if the dream is held close to the heart, and imagination is applied to what there is close at hand, everything is still possible.

But wait! Some cynic from the edge of the crowd insists that human beings still *can't really* fly. Not like birds, anyway. True. But somewhere in some little garage, some maniac with a gleam in his eye is scarfing vitamins and mineral supplements, and practicing flapping his arms faster and faster.

*T*HE FIRST TIME WAS AT AUNT VIOLET'S apartment on Embassy Row in Washington, D.C., the summer I turned thirteen. I had come by train all the way from Waco, Texas, to visit the Big City on the Potomac. Aunt Violet was a hard-core social climber, a lovable snob, an aspiring gourmet—and she thought my mother was a twit. All of which endeared Aunt Violet to me. Aunt Violet and I got along just fine. Until the night of the Big Dinner.

The lineup included a senator, a couple of generals, and assorted foreigners with their assorted ladies. A very large deal, indeed, for a kid from Waco who had been upholstered for the occasion by Aunt Violet with a striped seersucker suit and a bow tie. *Très chic!* Glorious me!

Anyhow. Having asked if I could help with dinner, I was handed a paper bag and told to wash the contents and slice them salad-thin. What was in the bag

was mushrooms. Frilly-edged, mottled-brown, dis-
eased-looking creepy things.

Now I had seen mushrooms and knew where they
grew. In dark slimy places in the cow barn and the
chicken yard at home. Once some grew out of a pair
of tennis shoes I left in my gym locker over the
summer. And fungus I knew because I had it between
my toes from wearing the same tennis shoes every
day for a year. But it had never occurred to me to
handle mushrooms, much less wash and slice and *eat*
them. *(My father told me Washington was a strange and
wicked place, and now I understood what he meant.)* So I
quietly put the whole bag down the trash chute,
thinking it was a joke on the country-boy-come-to-
the-city.

Guess they must have been *some* mushrooms, con-
sidering how old Aunty Violet carried on when she
found out. To this day I'm convinced that's why she
left me out of her will when she died. I had no class.
I confess that I still regard mushrooms and mushroom eaters with a good deal of suspicion. Oh, I've
acquired the necessary veneer of pretentious sophis-
tication all right—enough to eat the things when invited out to eat and to keep my opinions to myself, so
I'm cool and all. But I still don't understand about
mushrooms and mushroom eaters—not entirely, anyhow.

In fact, there's a whole lot of things I don't understand about entirely—some large, some small. I keep a list, and the list gets longer and longer as I get older and older. For example, here's a few mysteries I added this year:

Why are grocery carts made with one wheel that has a mind of its own and runs cockeyed to the other three?

Why do so many people close their eyes when they brush their teeth?

Why do people believe that pushing an elevator button several times will make the car come quicker?

Why can't we just spell it "orderves" and get it over with?

Why do people drop a letter in the mailbox and then open the lid again to see if it really went down?

Why are there zebras?

Why do people put milk cartons back into the fridge with just a tiny bit of milk left in the bottom?

Why aren't there any traditional Halloween carols?

Why does every tree seem to have one old stubborn leaf that just won't let go?

Is the recent marketing of cologne for dogs a sign of anything?

I know. Those aren't what you'd call industrial-strength mysteries. All the big-ticket things I don't understand are at the beginning of the list, and have been for a long time. Things like electricity and how homing pigeons do what they do and why you can't get to the end of rainbows. And even further up toward the beginning of the list of things I don't understand are the real big ones. Like why people laugh and what art is really for and why God doesn't fix some things or finish the job. And at the top of the list is why is there life, anyway, and how come I have to die?

Which brings me back to the subject of mushrooms. They were in this salad I was served for New Year's dinner, and I got to wondering about mushrooms again. So I got the encyclopedia out and read up on them a little. Fungi they are—the fruiting body, the sporophore of fungi. The dark underworld of living things—part of death, disease, decay, rot. Things that make their way in the world by feeding upon decaying matter. Yeast, smuts, mildews, molds, mushrooms— maybe one hundred thousand different kinds, maybe more, nobody knows for sure.

They're everywhere. In the soil, the air, in lakes, seas, river, rain, in food and clothing, inside you and me and everybody else—doing their thing. Without fungi there's not the loaf of bread or the jug of wine or even thou. Bread, wine, cheese, beer, good company, rare steaks, fine cigars—all moldy. The fungi, says the big book, "are responsible for the disintegration of organic matter and the release into the soil or atmosphere of the carbon, oxygen, nitrogen, and phosphorus that would forever be locked up in dead plants and animals and all people as well." Fungi— midwives between death and life and death and life again and again and yet again.

There is a terrible and wondrous truth working here. Namely, that all things live only if something else is cleared out of the path to make way. No death; no life. No exceptions. Things must come and go. People. Years. Ideas. Everything. The wheel turns, and the old is cleared away as fodder for the new.

And I picked at the mushrooms in that New Year's salad and ate them with respect if not enthusiasm. Wondering at what is going and coming. Quietly awed into silence by what I understand but cannot tell. Borne by grace downstream where I see but cannot say.

V. P. MENON WAS A SIGNIFICANT political figure in India during its struggle for independence from Britain after World War II. He was the highest-ranking Indian in the viceregal establishment, and it was to him that Lord Mountbatten turned for the final drafting of the charter plan for independence. Unlike most of the leaders of the independence movement, Menon was a rarity—a self-made man. No degree from Oxford or Cambridge graced his office walls, and he had no caste or family ties to support his ambitions.

Eldest son of twelve children, he quit school at thirteen and worked as a laborer, coal miner, factory hand, merchant, and schoolteacher. He talked his way into a job as a clerk in the Indian administration, and his rise was meteoric—largely because of his integrity and brilliant skills in working with both Indian and British officials in a productive way. Both Nehru and Mountbatten mentioned his name with highest praise as one who made practical freedom possible for his country.

Two characteristics stood out as particularly memorable—a kind of aloof, impersonal efficiency, and a reputation for personal charity. His daughter explained the background of this latter trait after he died. When Menon arrived in Delhi to seek a job in government, all his possessions, including his money and I.D., were stolen at the railroad station. He would have to return home on foot, defeated. In desperation he turned to an elderly Sikh, explained his troubles, and asked for a temporary loan of fifteen rupees to tide him over until he could get a job. The Sikh gave him the money. When Menon asked for his address so that he could repay the man, the Sikh said that Menon owed the debt to any stranger who came to him in need, as long as he lived. The help came from a stranger and was to be repaid to a stranger.

Menon never forgot that debt. Neither the gift of trust nor the fifteen rupees. His daughter said that the day before Menon died, a beggar came to the family home in Bangalore asking for help to buy new sandals, for his feet were covered with sores. Menon asked his daughter to take fifteen rupees out of his wallet to give to the man. It was Menon's last conscious act.

This story was told to me by a man whose name I do not know. He was standing beside me in the Bombay airport at the left-baggage counter. I had come to reclaim my bags and had no Indian currency left. The agent would not take a traveler's check, and I was uncertain about getting my luggage and making my plane. The man paid my claim-check fee—about eighty cents—and told me the story as a way of refusing my attempt to figure out how to repay him. His father had been Menon's assistant and had learned Menon's charitable ways and passed them on to his son. The son had continued the tradition of seeing himself in debt to strangers, whenever, however.

From a nameless Sikh to an Indian civil servant to his assistant to his son to me, a white foreigner in a moment of frustrating inconvenience. The gift was not large as money goes, and my need was not great, but the spirit of the gift is beyond price and leaves me blessed and in debt.

On several occasions when I have thought about the story of the Good Samaritan, I have wondered about the rest of the story. What effect did the charity have on the man who was robbed and beaten and taken care of by the Good Samaritan? Did he remember the cruelty of the robbers and shape his life with that memory? Or did he remember the nameless generosity of the Samaritan and shape his life with that debt? What did he pass on to the strangers in his life, those in need he met?

THE BIG DEAL OF MY SUMMER was a week in Weiser, Idaho.

Maybe that's hard to believe. Because if you've ever looked at an Idaho map, you know Weiser is nowhere. But if you play the fiddle, Weiser, Idaho, is the center of the universe. The Grand National Old Time Fiddlers' Contest is there the last week in June. And since I've fiddled around some in my time, I went.

Four thousand people live there in normal times. Five thousand more come out of the bushes and trees and hills for the contest. The town stays open around the clock, with fiddling in the streets, dancing at the VFW hall, fried chicken in the Elks Lodge, and free camping at the rodeo grounds.

People from all over show up—fiddlers from Pottsboro, Texas; Sepulpa, Oklahoma; Thief River Falls, Minnesota; Caldwell, Kansas; Three Forks, Montana;

and just about every other little crossroads town you care to mention. And even Japan!

It used to be that the festival was populated by country folks—pretty straight types—short hair, church on Sunday, women in their place, and all that. Then the long-haired hippie freaks began to show up. The trouble was that the freaks could fiddle to beat hell. And that's all there was to it.

So, the town turned over the junior high school and its grounds to the freaks. The contest judges were put in an isolated room where they could only hear the music. Couldn't see what people looked like or what their names were—just the fiddling. As one old gentleman put it, "Son, I don't care if you're stark nekkid and wear a bone in your nose. If you kin fiddle, you're all right with me. It's the music we make that counts."

So I was standing there in the middle of the night in the moonlight in Weiser, Idaho, with about a thousand other people who were picking and singing and fiddling together—some with bald heads, some with hair to their knees, some with a joint, some with a long-necked bottle of Budweiser, some with beads, some with Archie Bunker T-shirts, some eighteen and some eighty, some with corsets and some with no bras, and the music rising like incense into the night toward whatever gods of peace and good-will there may be. I was standing there, and this policeman—a real honest-to-god Weiser policeman who is standing next to me and *picking a banjo (really, I swear it)*—says to me, "Sometimes the world seems like a fine place, don't it?"

Oh, yes, and yet again, yes. Yes, indeed.

Pick it, brother, let the music roll on. . . .

SAN DIEGO HAS A ZOO and wild-animal park—the finest in the world, some say. Being a serious zoo fan, I spent a day there recently. Zoos are great for adults—they take your mind off reality for a while.

For example, did you ever look real close at a giraffe? A giraffe is unreal. If there is a heaven and I go there (*don't bet heavy on either of those*), but *if*, then one thing I'm going to ask about is giraffes.

Little girl standing beside me at the zoo asked her mommy the question I had: "What's it for?" Mommy didn't know. Does the giraffe know what he's for? Or care? Or even think about his place in things? A giraffe has a black tongue twenty-seven inches long and no vocal cords. A giraffe has nothng to say. He just goes on giraffing.

Besides the giraffe, I saw a wombat, a duck-billed platypus, and an orangutan. Unreal. The orangutan looked just like my uncle Woody. Uncle Woody is pretty unreal, too. He belongs in a zoo. That's what his wife says. And that makes me wonder what it would be like if samples of *people* were also in zoos.

I was thinking about that last notion while watching the lions. A gentleman lion and six lady lions. Looks like a real nice life being in a zoo. The lions are so prolific that the zoo has had to place IUDs in each of the lionesses. So all the lions do is eat and sleep and scratch fleas and have sex without consequences. The zoo provides food, lodging, medical care, old-age security, and funeral expenses. Such a deal.

We humans make a big thing about our being the only thinking, reflective critter, and make proclamations like "the unexamined life is not worth living." But I look at the deal the giraffes and lions and wombats and duck-billed-what's-its have, and I think I could go for the unexamined life. If the zoo ever needs me, I'd give it a try. I certainly qualify as a one-of-a-kind endangered species. And examining my life sure gets to be a drag sometimes.

Can't you imagine you and your kids passing by a large, comfy cage, all littered with cigar butts, cognac bottles, and T-bone steak bones—and there, snoozing in the sun, is old Fulghum with six beautiful ladies piled up around him. And your kid points and says, "What's it for?" And I'd yawn and open one eye and say, "Who cares?" Like I say, zoos tend to take your mind off reality.

The lion and the giraffe and the wombat and the rest do what they do and are what they are. And somehow manage to make it there in the cage, living the unexamined life. But to be human is to know and care and ask. To keep rattling the bars of the cage of existence hollering, "What's it for?" at the stones and stars, and making prisons and palaces out of the echoing answers. That's what we do and that's what we are. And that's why a zoo is a nice place to visit but I wouldn't want to live there.

THIS IS CALLED "THE MYSTERY OF TWENTY-FIFTH Avenue, Northeast." It has semi-cosmic implications. It's about the fact that we once lived at the dead end of a dead-end street, two blocks long, at the bottom of a hill.

It wasn't much of a street to look at in the first place. I mean, it really didn't *call* to you to come down it. Kind of narrow and crooked and cluttered up. Ed Weathers's van and his brother's GMC two-ton flatbed, and the Dillses' old Airstream trailer were just part of the vehicular obstacle course. Still, you could see all the way down from Ninety-fifth to the end of it.

And there were two signs up there at Ninety-fifth, too—one on each side of the street. Big yellow and black signs. Both said the same thing: STREET ENDS. And down here at our end of the street was another sign, a big sign. Black and white, with stripes and reflectors and all. DEAD END is what it said. Right in the middle of the end of the street it said that. And you could see it for a long way off.

Well, for *all* that, people just drove on down the street anyway. Not just part way, mind you. Not just to where the reality of the situation cleared up. No, sir. They drove all the way down, right up to the sign, the big black one with stripes, the one that said DEAD END.

And they read that sign two or three times. As if they were foreigners and had to translate the English. They looked on either side of the sign to see if there was a way around it. Sometimes they sat there for two or three minutes adjusting their minds. Then they backed up and tried turning around as close to the sign as possible. Backing and filling between our yard and Mrs. Paulski's marigold bed and the blackberry bushes across the street, running over some of each. Funny thing is that once they got turned around, they never drove away slow and thoughtful—as if they'd learned something. No, they tore away at full throttle, as if fleeing evil. There's no pattern. All kinds of hoopies, all kinds of people, broad daylight and pitch dark. Even a police car a couple of times, and once a fire truck.

Innate skepticism or innate stupidity? I confess I do not know. A psychiatrist friend tells me it's a sample of an unconscious need to deny—that everyone wants

the road or The Way to continue *on* instead of ending.
So you drive as far as you can, even when you can
clearly read the sign. You want to think you are
exempt, that it doesn't apply to you. But it does.

Now I was wondering. If I had printed that up and
then put little copies in a little box and attached it to
the sign that said DEAD END, with a smaller note that
said "Free Information Explaining Why You Are
Here—Take One" . . . if I had done that, would people have read it? Would it have made any difference?
Would they have been more careful of the lawn and
the marigolds and the blackberry bushes? Would they
have driven away any slower?

Or maybe I should have put up a sign at the top of
the hill that said WAYSIDE SHRINE AT END OF STREET—
COME ON DOWN AND CONFRONT THE ULTIMATE
MEANING OF LIFE. What effect would that have had on
traffic?

If I had done that, would I have become a famous
guru? Swami Deadendus?

We moved, so I'll never know.

A TROUBLED MAN PAID A VISIT TO HIS RABBI. A wise and good old rabbi, as all rabbis try to be. "Rabbi," said he, wringing his hands, "I am a failure. More than half the time I do not succeed in doing what I must do."

"Oh?" said the rabbi.

"Please say something wise, rabbi," said the man.

After much pondering, the rabbi spoke as follows: "Ah, my son, I give you this wisdom: Go and look on page 930 of *The New York Times Almanac* for the year 1970, and you will find peace of mind maybe."

"Ah," said the man, and he went away and did that thing.

Now this is what he found: The listing of the lifetime batting averages of all the greatest baseball players. Ty Cobb, the greatest slugger of them all, had a lifetime average of only .367. Even Babe Ruth didn't do so good.

So the man went back to the rabbi and said in a questioning tone: "Ty Cobb—.367—that's it?"

"Right," said the rabbi. "Ty Cobb—.367. He got a hit once out of every three times at bat. He didn't even bat .500—so what can *you* expect already?"

"Ah," said the man, who thought he was a wretched failure because only half the time he did not succeed at what he must do.

Theology is amazing, and holy books abound.

I WAS JUST WONDERING. Did you ever go to somebody's house for dinner or a party or something and then use the bathroom? And while you were in there, did you ever take a look around in the medicine cabinet? Just to kind of compare notes, you know? Didn't you ever—just look around a little?

I have a friend who does it all the time. He's doing research for a Ph.D. in sociology. He says lots of other people do it, too. And they aren't working on a Ph.D. in sociology, either. It's not something people talk about much—because you think you might be the only one who is doing it, and you don't want people to think you're strange, right?

My friend says if you want to know the truth about people, it's the place to go. All you have to do is look in the drawers and shelves and cabinets in the bathroom. And take a look at the robes and pajamas and nightgowns hanging on the hook behind the door. You'll get the picture. He says all their habits and hopes and dreams and sorrows, illnesses and hang-ups, and even their sex life—all stand revealed in that one small room.

He says most people are secret slobs. He says the deepest mysteries of the race are tucked into the nooks and crannies of the bathroom, where we go to be alone, to confront ourselves in the mirror, to comb and curry and scrape and preen our hides, to coax our aging and ailing bodies into one more day, to clean ourselves and relieve ourselves, to paint and deodor-ize our surfaces, to meditate and consult our oracle and attempt to improve our lot.

He says it's all there. In cans and bottles and tubes and boxes and vials. Potions and oils and unguents and sprays and tools and lotions and perfumes and appliances and soaps and pastes and pills and creams and pads and powders and medicines and devices beyond description—some electric and some not. The wonders of the ages.

He says he finds most bathrooms are about the same, and it gives him a sense of the wondrous unity of the human race.

I don't intend to start an epidemic of spelunking in people's bathrooms. But I did just go in and take a look in my own. I get the picture. I don't know whether to laugh or cry.

Take a look. In your own. And from now on, please go to the bathroom before you visit me. Mine is closed to the public.

DESPITE SWEARING I WOULD NEVER DO IT, I went to the thirty-year reunion of my high school class, deep in the heart of Texas. I had not seen those "kids" since the night I graduated.

And one quick glance confirmed my worst expectations. Bald heads, gray hair, wrinkles, fat, liver marks.

Old. We're *old* now, thought I. So soon. And it's all downhill from here. Decay, rot, disease, an early grave. I felt tired. I began to walk slower, with a noticeable limp. I began to think about my will and make mental notes for my funeral.

This malaise lasted all of thirty seconds. Wiped out by the bright memory of two men I had met earlier in the summer at a truck stop in Burns, Oregon.

Mr. Fred Easter, sixty-eight, and his good friend, Mr. Leroy Hill, sixty-two. They were bicycling from Pismo Beach, California, to see the rodeo in Calgary, Alberta. They had been sitting on a bench by the beach, reading in the newspaper about the rodeo, and one of them said, "Let's go!" and they got up and went. And here they were in Burns in flashy riding suits, with high-tech bikes and all. When I asked Mr. Easter how come, he laughed. "Why, just for the hell of it, son. Just for the bloody hell of it!"

Fifty-eight hundred miles later, via Colorado and the Grand Canyon, they expect to arrive home in October, unless, of course, other interesting things turn up along the way. They are not in a race.

I walked away from that encounter tall and straight and handsome and young—making new lists of all the things I would do and all the places I would go and all the things I would *be* in all the years ahead of me.

Look for me at the rodeo in Calgary in the year 2004. You'll recognize me by the bicycle bearing the sign PISMO BEACH OR BUST!

A SUMMER'S EVENING. The front porch of my grandfather's farmhouse. By the light of an aged and sputtering lantern, I am playing a cutthroat game of Old Maid with five cardsharks under the age of ten. Nephews and their friends. I am the "babysitter," from my point of view, and the latest "sucker" to play cards with them, as they see it.

We are eating popcorn laced with grape jelly, and knocking back straight shots of milk right out of the carton, which is being solemnly passed from hand to hand. We're all wearing cowboy hats and chewing on kitchen matches, picking our teeth. That's the rule— hats and toothpicks—you must look *serious* when you play cards.

And these are hard-core bull-goose card whippers. I have been the Old Maid three times running, and am down to nine M&M's and four pennies in my pot. We are all cheating every chance we get. One of them has an extra deck and is passing cards under the table. I can't prove it, but that's what I think. Anyhow, what saved me from utter ruin at the hands of this criminal element was moths.

A flock of moths were corkscrewing around the Coleman lantern. Every once in a while one would hit the hot spot and go *zzssshh* and spin out and crash like a fighter plane in a bad combat movie. Finally, one zerked out of orbit into the nearest spider's web, and the spider mugged, rolled, wrapped, and sucked the life-juice out of this poor moth so fast and so mercilessly it stopped the Old Maid game dead. A Green Beret ranger could learn something about the garrote from this eight-legged acrobat with the poison mouth.

The kids loved it. Encouraged by this homicidal scene, one of the boys leaves the table, rolls up a sheet of newspaper, and starts a king-hell massacre on the rest of the circling moths. Knocking them out of the air like a heavy hitter at batting practice, and then smashing them flat on the table, leaving little furry smudges and broken parts.

I leapt to the defense of the moths. It's bad enough that the lantern hypnotizes them into kamikaze runs and that spiders zap them into lunch meat, but small boys with newspapers are excessive handicaps to have to overcome.

"Why're you killing the poor moths?"

"Moths are *bad*," says he.

"Everybody knows *that*," shouts another.

"Sure, moths *eat* your clothes."

I could not sway them. *All* moths are *bad*. *All* butterflies are *good*. Period. Moths and butterflies are not the same thing. Moths sneak around in the dark munching your sweater and are ugly. Butterflies hang out with flowers in the daytime and are pretty. Never mind any facts or what silkworm moths are responsible for, or what poisonous butterflies do. With a firmness that would have made John Calvin proud, moths were condemned, now and forevermore, amen. Out of the mouths of babes may come gems of wisdom, but also garbage.

That ended the Old Maid game. I stomped off, telling them I wouldn't play cards with killers, and they shouted they wouldn't play with someone who ate all the grape jelly while nobody was looking. I went to bed thinking if the future is in the hands of maniacs like these, we're in trouble.

The next morning the youngest came to me with a large dead moth in one hand and a magnifying glass in the other. "Look" says he, "this moth looks like a little teddy bear with wings and feathers on its head."

"You like teddy bears?" I ask.

"Yes, I like teddy bears."

"You like small flying teddy bears with feathers on their head?"

"Yes," says he, "I think I do."

Once again I was the Old Maid.

One must, sometimes at least, practice what one preacheth, and if one should look at moths without prejudice and with grace, one may be forced to consider small boys in a somewhat more generous light. Some moths make silk. Some small boys make sense.

MY GRANDFATHER SAM CALLED ME UP last Tuesday to ask me if I'd take him to a football game. Grandfather likes small-town high school football— and even better, the eight-man ball played by crossroads teams. Grandfather is a fan of amateurs and small scale. Some people are concerned about how it is that good things happen to bad people, and there are those concerned about how bad things happen to good people. But my grandfather is interested in those times when *miracles* happen to ordinary people. Here again, he likes small scale.

When a nothing team full of nothing kids from a nothing town rises up with nothing to lose against some upmarket suburban outfit with new uniforms, and starts chucking hail-Mary bombs from their own goal line, and their scrawny freshman tight end catches three in a row to win the game—well, it does your heart good.

Murphy's Law does not always hold, says Grandfather Sam. Every once in a while the fundamental laws of the universe seem to be momentarily suspended, and not only does everything go right, nothing seems to be able to keep it from going right. It's not always something as dramatic as the long bomb or the slam-dunk that wins ball games.

Ever drop a glass in the sink when you're washing dishes and have it bounce nine times and not even chip? Ever come out after work to find your lights have been on all day and your battery's dead but you're parked on a hill and you let your old hoopy roll and it fires the first time you pop the clutch and off you roar with a high heart? Ever pull out that drawer in your desk that has a ten-year accumulation of junk in it—pull it too far and too fast—and just as it's about to vomit its contents all over the room you get a knee under it and stagger back hopping on one foot doing a balancing act like the Great Zucchini and you don't lose it? A near-miss at an intersection; the glass of knocked-over milk that waltzes across the table but doesn't spill; the deposit that beat your rubber check to the bank because there was a holiday you forgot about; the lump in your breast that turned out to be benign; the heart attack that turned out to be gas; picking the right lane for once in a traffic jam; opening the door of your car with a coat hanger through the wing window on the first try. And on and on and on and on.

When small miracles occur for ordinary people, day by ordinary day. When not only did the worst not happen, but maybe nothing much happened at all, or some little piece fell neatly into place. The grace of what-might-have-been-but-wasn't, and it was good to get off scot-free for once. The ecstasy of what-could-never-happen-but-did, and it was grand to have beat the odds against for a change. Or the bliss of just what-was-for-a-day when nothing special took place—life just worked.

My grandfather says he blesses God each day when he takes himself off to bed having *eaten* and not having *been eaten* once again. "Now I lay me down to sleep. In the peace of amateurs, for whom so many blessings flow. I thank you, God, for what went right! Amen."

WE HAVE BECOME CATALOG JUNKIES. My sweet wife and I. Once you get on one list, you get them all. Especially in autumn they choke the mailbox, and we dutifully leaf through them by the fire after supper, amazed at all the neat stuff we don't have and never knew existed. It's getting to be like the old days when the latest Sears catalog showed up to fuel the flames of the desire for more stuff.

She asked me what do I not have that I *really* want. I didn't tell her everything that came to mind, but once I set aside the more ludicrous notions involving lust, gluttony, and wanton greed, the discussion turned in a more meaningful direction:

I'd like to be able to see the world through somebody else's mind and eyes for just one day.

There's a morning in the summer of 1984 I'd like to live over just as it was.

I'd like to speak ten foreign languages well enough to get the humor of another culture.

I'd like to talk with Socrates and watch Michelangelo sculpt "David."

And so on and so forth. You get the drift of the conversation, and it went well into the night. And none of it could be had from catalogs. These were desires made out of nostalgia and imagination, packed in the boxes that dreams come out of.

Most of all, most of all, I'd like to have a living grandfather. Both of mine are mysteries to me. My father's father was shot to death in a saloon in Texas in 1919. In the same year, my mother's father walked out of the house one morning on his way to work and never came back. I still don't know why, and those who know don't say. In the fairy-tale factory in my mind, I imagine that *if* I had a grandfather, he'd be old and wise and truly grand. A bit of the philosopher, a bit of the magician, and something of a shaman.

He would have called me up this week and asked me if I had heard the news about the photograph of a new solar system. Existing around a star twice as big and ten times as bright as our own sun—a star named Beta Pictoris. And around that star is a vast swarm of solid particles in a disk forty billion miles in diameter. And some of those particles are probably planets. All of it about fifty light-years from earth. Way, *way* out there. My grandfather would say I should come get him, and we'd go out and look at the stars and stay up all night and talk.

We'd see Venus and Jupiter almost in conjunction

with the bright star Lambda Sagittarii. The great winged horse of Pegasus riding high in the southwest sky. The misty patch of the Andromeda Galaxy almost overhead. And the Milky Way swung around since summer to run east and west. A shooting star would set my grandfather to talking about seeing Halley's Comet in 1910, and how the night of May 18–19 he witnessed what was probably the largest simultaneously shared event in human history. And how the world was divided between those who celebrated and those who watched in fear and trembling. My grandfather would make me promise to watch the return of Halley's Comet the next time around, on his behalf.

Along toward dawn we would talk of Orion, the Great Hunter, dominating the sky overhead. With the stars Betelgeuse and Bellatrix, the nebula in the belt, and Rigel and Saiph in the feet, pointing toward Sirius, the brighest star in the heavens. And we'd talk about how human beings have been looking at the very same stars and thinking the same things for so long. And how there must be life up there, same as here, and whatever it's like, it's looking at us. Do we shine? Are we part of some pattern in somebody else's night sky—a projection of their imaginations and wonderings? My grandfather would say he was sure it was so. My grandfather would say we're part of something incredibly wonderful—more marvelous than we imagine or can imagine. My grandfather would say we ought to go out and look at it once in a while so we don't lose our place in it. And then my grandfather would go to bed.

You'd like my grandfather. And he'd like you, I think. Happy Grandfather's Day to him, wherever he is. If you see him, let him take you out to see the stars some night.

And tell him I said I'd really like it if he came home for Christmas.

*I*T'S A LITTLE UNCOMFORTABLE FOR ME, telling you about my grandfather. He does and does not exist— it depends on what "real" is. You may be a little confused about what I've told you. *I* certainly am. I suppose it's harmless enough for a yearning to be so strong that what you need becomes very real in some corner of your heart. Picassso said, "Everything you can imagine is real." And I understand that.

In a sense we make up all our relatives, though. Fathers, mothers, brothers, sisters, and the rest. Especially if they are dead or distant. We take what we know, which isn't ever the whole story, and we add it to what we wish and need, and stitch it together into some kind of family quilt to wrap up in on our mental couch.

We even make ourselves up, fusing what we are with what we wish into what we must become. I'm not sure why it must be so, but it is. It helps to know this. Thinking about the grandfather I *wish* I *had* prepares me for the grandfather I *wish to be*, a way of using what I am to shape the best that is to come. It is a preparation.

Sometime, not too far from now, a child will call out "Grandfather," and I will know what to do.

*T*HERE IS A PERSON WHO HAS PROFOUNDLY disturbed my peace of mind for a long time. She doesn't even know me, but she continually goes around minding my business. We have very little in common. She is an old woman, an Albanian who grew up in Yugoslavia; she is a Roman Catholic nun who lives in poverty in India. I disagree with her on fundamental issues of population control, the place of women in the world and in the church, and I am turned off by her naïve statements about "what God wants." She stands at the center of great contradictory notions and strong forces that shape human destiny. She drives me crazy. I get upset every time I hear her name or read her words or see her face. I don't even want to talk about her.

In the studio where I work, there is a wash basin. Above the wash basin is a mirror. I stop at this place several times each day to tidy up and look at myself in the mirror. Alongside the mirror is a photograph of the troublesome woman. Each time I look in the mirror at myself, I also look at her face. In it I have seen more than I can tell; and from what I see, I understand more than I can say.

The photograph was taken in Oslo, Norway, on the tenth of December, in 1980. This is what happened there:

A small, stooped woman in a faded blue sari and worn sandals received an award. From the hand of a king. An award funded from the will of the inventor of dynamite. In a great glittering hall of velvet and gold and crystal. Surrounded by the noble and famous in formal black and in elegant gowns. The rich, the powerful, the brilliant, the talented of the world in attendance. And there at the center of it all—a little old lady in sari and sandals. Mother Teresa, of India. Servant of the poor and sick and dying. To her, the Nobel Peace Prize.

No shah or president or king or general or scientist or pope; no banker or merchant or cartel or oil company or ayatollah holds the key to as much power as she has. None is as rich. For hers is the invincible weapon against the evils of this earth: the caring heart. And hers are the everlasting riches of this life: the wealth of the compassionate spirit.

To cut through the smog of helpless cynicism, to take only the tool of uncompromising love; to make manifest the capacity for healing humanity's wounds; to make the story of the Good Samaritan a living reality; and to live so true a life as to shine out from the back streets of Calcutta takes courage and faith we cannot admit in ourselves and cannot be without.

I do not speak her language. Yet the eloquence of her life speaks to me. And I am chastised and blessed at the same time. I do not believe one person can do much in this world. Yet there she stood, in Oslo, affecting the world around. I do not believe in her version of God. But the power of her faith shames me. And I believe in Mother Teresa.

December in Oslo. The message for the world at Christmastide is one of peace. Not the peace of a child asleep in the manger of long ago. Nor the peace of a full dinner and a nap by the fire on December 25. But a tough, vibrant, vital peace that comes from the extraordinary gesture one simple woman in a faded sari and worn sandals makes this night. A peace of mind that comes from a piece of work.

Some years later, at a grand conference of quantum physicists and religious mystics at the Oberoi Towers Hotel in Bombay, I saw that face again. Standing by the door at the rear of the hall, I sensed a presence beside me. And there she was. Alone. Come to speak to the conference as its guest. She looked at me and smiled. I see her face still.

She strode to the rostrum and changed the agenda

of the conference from intellectual inquiry to moral activism. She said, in a firm voice to the awed assembly: "We can do no great things; only small things with great love."

The contradictions of her life and faith are nothing compared to my own. And while I wrestle with frustration about the impotence of the individual, she goes right on changing the world. While I *wish* for more power and resources, she *uses* her power and resources to do what she can do at the moment.

She upsets me, disturbs me, shames me. *What does she have that I do not?*

If ever there is truly peace on earth, goodwill to men, it will be because of women like Mother Teresa. Peace is not something you *wish* for; it's something you *make,* something you *do,* something you *are,* and something you *give away*!

My FAVORITE BOOK ENDING is no ending at all. It's where James Joyce leaves off in *Finnegans Wake,* in midsentence, without punctuation or explanation. Some scholars believe the last phrase connects with the incomplete sentence that begins the book, implying an unending cycle. I hope it's so. I like that. But Joyce never said. You are free to draw your own conclusions.

On a smaller scale, all this reminds me of the hours I spent trying to tell bedtime stories to my oldest son. Before I got the bare beginnings out of my mouth, he would want to know what happened *before* the story began, and as you might expect, no matter how conclusive and apocalyptic a story ending might be, a sleepy, squeaky voice would plead from out of the darkness, "And *then* what happened, Daddy?"

Back there at the beginning of this book I spoke of the question from the literary agent that set all this in motion: Did I have anything else I had written? Yes. The question much later was: And is there still more? The answer is yes, again. A lot more. And the writing goes on as I go on.

But this is a place to pause. If the fabric of existence is truly seamless, the weavers still must sleep.

The next time I will tell you about frogs; Miss Emily Phipps; a sign in a grocery store in Pocatello, Idaho; the most disastrous wedding of all time; a Greek phrase, *asbestos gelos* (unquenchable laughter); the Salvation Navy; the man who knew then what he knows now; the smallest circus in the world; the truth about high school; and the time when the bed was on fire when I lay down on it; and